Ghosts o
West Country

Beau Nash

Ghosts of the West Country

Keith B. Poole

JARROLD

ACKNOWLEDGEMENTS

I must express my gratitude to libraries and librarians, who have been most helpful, especially in the West Country; to local historians, newspapers and magazines; also to the many authorities dealing with the subject.

I must also express my warmest thanks to Roberta Sharpe for courtesy, care and understanding in dealing with long-standing problems; appreciation is due to my editor Donald Greig for his encouragement, and to Clare Shaw for her careful handling of the text.

Lastly, deep gratitude to my wife, Madeline, for endless patience, constant care and help in all things concerned with the manuscript.

Keith B. Poole is the author of many ghost books and has contributed short stories to New Writing and Penguin New Writing. As a local historian, he has published many hundreds of articles in regional newspapers and magazines. An Honorary Fellow of the Heraldry Society, he is a university extramural lecturer in Heraldry, Genealogy and Medieval History and lectures in these subjects for the National Association of Decorative and Fine Arts Societies. He lives in Cornwall.

Further books by the author:
Historic Heraldic Families
The Two Beaux (Beau Nash and Beau Brummel)
Ghosts of Wessex
Britain's Haunted Heritage
Unfamiliar Spirits
Great British Families – their legends and traditions

Cover illustration: public hanging after the Monmouth Rebellion, as decreed by the infamous Judge Jeffreys.

CONTENTS

INTRODUCTION 7

AVON 9
    Bristol's House of Fear *(Stoke Bishop, nr Clifton Down)* ...10
    The Black Monk *(All Saints Vicarage, Bristol)* 12
    The White Lady of the Manor *(Stapleton Manor)* 13
    The Ghosts of Bath 15

CORNWALL
    The Death Dream *(Scorrier House, nr Redruth)* 21
    Three Rare Ghosts *(Perranzabuloe, Looe, Launceston)* ...23
    The Most Evil Ghost *(Bodmin area)* 27
    The Haunted Church and Manor House *(Poundstock)* 30
    The Tormented Spirit *(Altarnun)* 34
    The Bodmin Moor Ghost 40

DEVON
    The Sinister Secret Room *(Chambercombe Manor)* 47
    The Visitation of 'Old Madam' *(Lew Trenchard)* 51
    The Dreaded Ghost House *(Sampford Peverell)* 54
    The Violent Castle Ghost *(Berry Pomeroy Castle)* 60
    The Beast of the Moors *(Exmoor)* 64

DORSET
    A Unique Ghost *(Beaminster)* 69
    The Ghost Sextet *(Athelhampton Hall, nr Puddletown)* ...71
    The Gruesome Ghost *(Tarrant Gunville)* 75
    The Screaming Skull *(Bettiscombe Manor House)* 77
    Another Evil Ghost 79

GLOUCESTERSHIRE
    The Haunted Mansion *(Woodchester Park)* 85
    Berkeley Castle 87

5

SOMERSET
    The Possessive Farmhouse Skull *(Chilton Cantelo)* 93
    The Ghost Train *(Kentsford)* 94
    The Arthurian Ghosts *(Cadbury Castle)* 96
    Ghosts and Gardens *(Tolland, nr Taunton)* 98
    A Very Dangerous Ghost *(Brockley)* 101
    One Night of Terror *(Kentsford)* .106

WILTSHIRE
    The Demon Drummer of Tedworth 111
    The Ghosts of Littlecote House 114
    Ghosts Galore in Longleat 117
    The Remorseful Ghost *(Marlborough)* 121

INTRODUCTION

Legends form the historic background of every nation, and ghost stories are an integral part of legends and folklore. The words 'ghost' and 'spirit' have been defined in detail by leading dictionaries, as has the word 'legend', their meaning changing dramatically with the centuries. In her historic book, *William the Silent*, Dr C. V. Wedgwood gives possibly the best interpretation of the word 'legend' when she says 'Legend is often symbolic of a whole atmosphere.' What could be more intense than the atmosphere created by story-tellers in the torch-lit halls of their patrons, in those far-off days before printing was invented and books became available, when men with splendid memories learned stories and legends and travelled the countryside, to be invited into candle-lit cottages to tell their tales? Centuries later the tradition continues in lonely Scottish islands where stories are told in Gaelic; in Arabia or Egypt where crowds of expectant listeners eagerly await the next part of a long serial about giants, dwarfs, spirits and dragons.

England is a country with strong beliefs in ghosts and spirits, and though comparatively few people have ever seen a ghost, many believe 'there must be something'. The author has twice seen a ghost and is curiously aware of unseen apparitions, as on the occasion he was unable to cross the drawbridge of Berry Pomeroy Castle, although he knew nothing until later of the tragedy that had occurred there (see page 60).

Librarians report that ghost books are extremely popular, and it would be interesting to know if fear is uppermost in the reactions of readers, because so many ghosts seem to return to a place where they were happy and contented rather than to cause disturbance and fear, as is more commonly believed. Indeed spirits can often bring joy to their beholders.

Sir Winston Churchill gave an impressive meaning to the word legend when in his great book *The History of the English-speaking People* he wrote:

> If we could see exactly what happened we should find ourselves in the presence of a theme as well founded, as inspired and as inalienable from the inheritance of mankind as the Odyssey or the Old Testament. It is all true, or it ought to be and more and better besides. And wherever men are fighting against barbarism, tyranny, and massacre, for freedom, law and honour, let them remember that the frame of their deeds, even though they themselves be exterminated, may perhaps be celebrated as long as the world rolls around.

The Garrick's Head Hotel, Bath

AVON

It would be difficult to say whether Bristol has more ghosts than Bath, but together they probably have more than any other area in the West Country. It is thanks to the *Clifton Chronicle* of various years that records of the principal ghost stories have been retained. On 24 November 1909, the paper recorded the story of a haunted house in Clifton Down. The writer, an American gentleman, had come with his wife in the winter of that year to see a well-furnished house in Bristol. The owner of the house lived in Bath, where the American couple were also staying, and he had advertised the house in a Bath paper. The couple liked the district and the house immediately, and quickly decided on renting it.

It was an old-fashioned house, which pleased the maids they at once engaged as much as their master and mistress, and they soon settled in. The American converted one of the rooms on the ground floor to a study. Nothing happened for many weeks until one day, while he was writing at his desk, he was suddenly disturbed by the sound of a child crying. When the crying became louder the noise got on his nerves, so much so that he went out to the maids' room, thinking the child belonged to one of them or to a visitor. To his astonishment they knew nothing at all about a child, nor had they heard the crying.

A few days later the American's wife sat writing a letter at the desk her husband used, but for some unknown reason felt so despondent and unhappy that she could not finish the letter. Both she and her husband were now greatly troubled and mystified, but were slightly comforted when for a whole week no one in the household was disturbed. The peace was suddenly shattered when loud and desperate sobbing broke out and continued at intervals for days. This time the maids all heard it as well. When a few days later they were paid a visit by the local clergyman, as a courtesy to new residents, the American felt obliged to tell his guest that there was something very wrong about the house – something inexplicable. One of the strange things about the story is that the priest made no offer to exorcise what was obviously a haunted house, even after he had been told about the crying child that was so badly affecting the whole household.

The crying became more and more frequent and disturbing, to such an extent that the American couple decided they could no longer live there. They returned to Bath to see the landlord and to terminate the lease, long before it was due to end, only to hear that the landlord had lived in the house himself for years before going to live in Bath, and neither he nor his family had ever been disturbed in any way.

BRISTOL'S HOUSE OF FEAR

Under this headline the *Clifton Chronicle* had at an earlier date recorded another frightening ghost story from a house at Stoke Bishop, near Clifton Down. So great was the terror in the house that it finally caused the death of the owner. In those days the district was almost uninhabited, for no traffic ran across the Downs and trams were still far in the future. People used Pitch and Pay Lane and Mariner's Lane, so that the house was well out in the country, which is why a Mr C. and his daughter Dorothy came to live there. The Paper used the pseudonym 'Mr C.' throughout the account rather than give his name. His daughter was fourteen years of age, he himself was an old man of seventy-three and a widower. The house was run by the housekeeper, a Miss B., who also looked after Dorothy, whom her father dearly, even obsessively loved.

As there was no school in the district Miss B. suggested it might be good for Dorothy to go to a good school as a boarder. Her father could not bear to part with her, but Dorothy herself, very lonely with no companions or any form of entertainment, told him she would like to go to school and make some friends. She had obviously been influenced by Miss B., and her father was almost forced to agree that she should go to school. Thus it was that a school was chosen and arrangements made for Dorothy to become a boarder and leave home in September, knowing they would not meet again until Christmas.

In October the maid they had engaged told the housekeeper that she had heard footsteps upstairs in one of the rooms, but that when she went up to look there was nobody in the room. The housekeeper told her that she must be dreaming for the room was empty, and it was probably the ivy rustling against the wall outside one of the windows. Towards the end of the month Mr C. was delighted to receive a letter from a very old friend asking if he might come and stay with him for a couple of days. He told the housekeeper to prepare Dorothy's room for his friend as it was the warmest room in the house. This she did.

In the morning when the guest came down to breakfast she asked him if he had slept well; he replied that he had not, having been disturbed by a child crying. He then asked if Dorothy were home and when told she was at school he became very puzzled, but asked the housekeeper not to mention anything to Mr C. Shortly after that another friend came as a guest and again the housekeeper was told to put her in Dorothy's room. She was a widow and a great friend of Mr C. and was concerned about his loneliness without his beloved Dorothy. When she came down the next morning she asked who was the fair-haired child who came into the room. 'I spoke to her,' she said, 'but she made no answer.' The housekeeper told her she must have been dreaming for there was no child in the house. Unfortunately she told Mr C. about the child and saw that he was greatly disturbed and anxious.

Strangely enough a third visitor had written to Mr C. to ask for his hospitality. He delightedly agreed and was distressed when after the first night she apologised to him and said she could not stay another night in the room. Mr C. was now so disturbed and afraid that he decided to sleep in Dorothy's room himself. He had not been asleep long before he was awakened by something sinister. His bed faced the dying fire and in the glow he saw a figure moving towards him. With a shock of fear and surprise he recognized Dorothy. She stood with her arms outstretched as if to embrace him, but as he spoke to her she vanished. The next morning, without mentioning his terrifying experience to Miss B., he ordered her to send a telegram to the school to ask if Dorothy was all right. He told Miss B. to go at once.

As Miss B. did not come back from the post office Mr C. became increasingly uneasy and suspicious, and his fears came to a head when the maid came to ask him if he knew that Miss B. had left her room in a great state of disorder. The drawers were all empty and all her papers, documents and personal jewellery had gone. In a state of great shock he scribbled out the words of a telegram addressed to the school and told his maid to send it off at once. Mr C. waited some hours for a reply but none came.

This time he himself left the house and managed to find a policeman, whom he asked to report his housekeeper's disappearance and his own suspicions and to try and get in touch with the school. A day or so later a detective called at the house for a full investigation of the case. Both men began a complete search upstairs and particularly in Dorothy's bedroom, but nothing was found until quite suddenly the detective trod on a creaking board and was immediately suspicious, convinced that it was the key to the mystery. Together they managed to prise open the floorboard and beneath it found the body of Dorothy. A doctor was summoned to come urgently, whose diagnosis was that the girl had been strangled, and possibly murdered in her sleep.

In spite of a widespread and continuous search for the housekeeper she was never discovered. The school had never recorded the name of Dorothy as a girl student. The shock of the loss of such a dearly loved daughter hastened Mr C's own death. The phantom was never seen again and the only possible reason for the murder seems to have been the housekeeper's intention to inherit all her master's estate, since there was no other member of his family still living. The *Clifton Chronicle* ended its account by saying that in spite of the terrible tragedy, new tenants had taken the house and had seen no sign of any ghost nor heard any bitter weeping from the phantom Dorothy.

THE BLACK MONK

In 1846 the *Bristol Times* published an article concerning the strange and mysterious rumours of ghostly activities around All Saints Vicarage on the corner of Corn Street and High Street, Bristol. The article was written in a derisive and sarcastic tone, starting with the words: 'We have this week a ghost story to relate. Yes, a real ghost story, and a ghost story without as yet any clue to its elucidation'. The building had originally been the ancient residence of the Guild of Calendarers, experts who indexed and analysed medieval documents. It had then been converted into a vicarage-house, and was still called so at that time although it was many years since any vicar had resided there. It was then occupied by a Mr and Mrs Jones, the sexton of the church and his wife, one or two lodgers and the servant-maid, who separately and jointly had begun to hear strange and inexplicable noises; worse still they had been visited nightly by a black monk who caused much terror to the inhabitants. The visitor could be heard walking about the house, and Mr Jones, by no means a nervous man, had become alarmed when he began to see flickering lights on the walls. His wife was equally frightened by the nightly noise of creaking shoes worn by a man wandering up and down the bedroom above her own, '…where no man was on the premises or ought to be. She was nearly killed with the fright.'

It was the servant-maid who had the worst shock when she saw the apparition push open her locked bedroom door one night. She had repeatedly had her bedroom door unbolted at night, between midnight and two o'clock, and had covered her head with her bed-quilt, too terrified to see the night prowler. But one night she saw him all the same, wearing something antique; 'lang syne gune,' she told the reporter; 'it was a whiskered gentleman who had gone to the length of shaking my bed and would have shaken me no doubt.'

When the story came to the ears of Mrs Crowe, author of *The Night Side of Nature*, she wrote to the *Bristol Times* for confirmation of the story, asking if there had been any solution. They replied, 'The whole affair is wrapped in the same mystery as when it was chronicled in the pages of the paper, subsequently confirmed by Mrs Jones.'

There were, however, other occupants of the house who had endured the same scares and anxieties and had seen and heard the same things as Mrs Jones. A black monk was described as the night prowler who beckoned to them to follow him through a bricked-up wall, and then vanished. Was this black monk perhaps someone who had hidden whatever he could, at the time of the Dissolution of the Monasteries and Religious Houses by Henry VIII in 1539? All Saints was considered then to be a West Country treasure house of gold, silver, and jewels, containing all the wealth of the Guild of Calendarers as well as their precious and ancient documents. So sure was Henry VIII that their treasures were there to be seized that he had the house ransacked twice without finding them.

THE WHITE LADY OF THE MANOR

When in the year 1854 Mrs Harford bought the 14th-century Stapleton Manor House near Bristol she was fully aware that it was haunted, because the owner had reduced the price so much in his anxiety to be rid of it and clearly welcomed her decision to buy it. In the magazine of that time called *All the Year Round* a full report of the mysterious White Lady was given. Mrs Harford, by asking local people before buying the house, had been told that the mysterious White Lady was a frequent nocturnal visitor, though nobody had seen her recently since the house had been empty for quite a long time. She had also been told by the landlord that noises had been heard within the panelling of one of the rooms both by day and by night, but neither did this deter Mrs Harford who moved in with her two sisters and servants. As the one large room upstairs had no panelling, only a papered wall, she decided there would be no noises there, and she and her elder sister installed themselves there in a huge four-poster bed, her younger sister occupying a bed beside them. In the main room, the salon, she felt all along the panelled walls and found them to be hollow, so that any of the reported noises might well have been caused by smugglers secreting their cargoes from the Revenue Officers.

For many months they were in no way disturbed, the house was peaceful and nothing suspicious occurred until in the middle of one night Mrs Harford was overcome by an uneasy feeling that there was someone in the room, though she herself always double-locked and bolted every room in the house before going to bed. To her astonishment she saw the diaphanous white figure of a lady dressed in a night-gown and old fashioned night-cap move slowly and purposefully across the room, past the foot of the bed and towards the windows. The figure was slight with fair hair, so like her own elder sister that she thought it must be her until slightly turning she saw that both her sisters were still sleeping peacefully. The figure suddenly vanished as Mrs Harford crept slowly out of the bed to examine the room and to see that all the doors and windows were securely locked, as indeed they were. She mentioned her experience the next day to her sisters and the maid but no one had heard or seen anything disturbing.

Curiously, some few years passed before the apparition appeared again to Mrs Harford. This time it was standing at the foot of the bed and gazed straight at her before vanishing, leaving her, for the first time, shocked and frightened. To her astonishment, when she spoke to a new servant that had recently come as a replacement, she discovered that she had not only seen the White Lady but had actually followed her as she glided rather than walked through the maid's own bedroom, through the door that led to a passage along which was her mistress's bedroom. The housekeeper, when told the story, said that the maid was imagining things and that the other maids would be leaving the house if they heard the story.

The other servants stayed on, although the one who had seen and followed the White Lady insisted that every detail of what she had said was the truth, and that anyway she did not believe in ghosts. Years passed and nothing more was seen or heard of the White Lady, nor did anyone discover who she was or why she had chosen the manor house. Like so many ghost stories she remains a mystery.

THE GHOSTS OF BATH

If one considers the antiquity of Bath it is surprising there are not many more haunted houses, inns, churchyards, or even a monastery, with more abundant records of ghostly activities. The three most important hauntings have taken place in the Garrick's Head Hotel and the adjoining Theatre Royal.

Amongst the many lesser known hauntings is that of 'The Man in a Black Hat', a daylight ghost who is said to have often been seen in the area. He also wears a long black cloak. He has been sketched and photographed, seen by day and by night walking the streets as well as standing in the now beautifully restored Assembly Rooms. He was very probably one of the first visitors to the building when it was built and is very happy to be in it again.

In a house in Whitcombe Terrace there is an evil and gruesome ghost, a terrifying old hag with a peculiarly shaped egg-domed head and mad staring eyes. She is dressed in almost ragged clothes that were once beautiful, and on one of her fingers she wears an opal ring. Her constant, dreadful appearances drove the owners out, leaving the house empty for years due to its evil reputation.

On the eve of the anniversary of the Battle of Lansdown, madly galloping horses have been heard, as well as the clashing of swords. In one of the rooms in a house in Edward Street, on a certain night in the year, the sounds of music and dancing feet can be heard performing old-fashioned waltzes. Immediately anyone opens the door they all vanish. There is a house in Gay Street, said to have often been haunted by voices from unseen people. Dr Samuel Johnson was a frequent visitor to take tea with Mrs Thrale, who owned the house in the eighteenth century. As both greatly enjoyed conversation the voices may have been the two of them talking, and more than likely other guests as well. Again, if anyone opened the door all sounds would cease. No one could be seen in the room.

The Garrick's Head Hotel, Bath

The most gruesome Bath haunting, however, was in York Villa. It was once the home of Frederick Duke of York, second son of George the Third. The Duke was a notorious libertine whose conduct provided the public with numerous scandals. He had brought his current mistress to York Villa, which in those days must have been a magnificent house. (All that remains of it today is used as a social club for a bus company's employees.) The Duke had by then already given his mistress children; whether she had had a quarrel with the Duke is not known, but he, calling an old and trusted retainer, told him to take charge of the children, as he himself was going to London and the lady had decided to follow him. Days passed into weeks and neither the Duke nor his mistress returned; the retainer became anxious. It seems that he himself had not continued to live in the Villa, but had delegated the care of the children to a woman he knew, though this is not known for certain. What is certain is the terrible shock he received when one day he went into the Villa to find that the woman and the staff of servants employed by the Duke were no longer there. He was struck down with a heart attack, and when the mistress finally returned she found not only the dead body of the retainer but the dead bodies of her children who had starved to death. For a long time afterwards the ghost of the retainer haunted the house as it wandered from room to room trying to put his guilty conscience to rest.

The Theatre Royal has one of the most unusual hauntings; it is a phantom butterfly of singular beauty, last seen in 1948 by a number of the audience of a Christmas pantomime, which contained a ballet in which the chorus girls were dressed as tortoiseshell butterflies. To the wonder and astonishment of the audience a real tortoiseshell butterfly was flicking about among the cast with as much pleasure as the dancers.

Another ghost of the Theatre Royal is the mysterious Grey Lady – a very mischievous phantom. Visitors to Bath have seen her both inside and outside the theatre and she has played many tricks on the occupants of the boxes. Once a play had a grandfather clock as part of the scenery which marked the time by its chimes. In one performance the clock continued its musical chime and had to be stopped by one of the actors. In another performance when it continued to chime past the appointed hour the Grey Lady herself stopped it. As late as 1975, when Dame Anna Neagle played the lead in *The Dame of Sark*, all the actors saw the Grey Lady, not just once but two or three times.

Theatre Royal, Bath

Theatre Royal, Bath

But it is the haunted Garrick's Head Hotel which has the most notorious ghosts. It was built in 1730 as a private gaming-house for the great Beau Nash, the monarch of Bath, as he was considered. It had a secret passage leading to the Theatre Royal, an escape route for gamblers if the house were raided, as gambling was illegal. Here there is yet another lady phantom, far more sinister, who in the year 1780 was the reason for a fierce quarrel breaking out between two gamblers in one of the rooms. Each had claimed the favours of the pretty lady, who was also in the room. Swords were drawn and oaths sworn as the duellists began to fight, one of them her lover. She fled in terror up the stairs to her own room. She heard a cry of victory from one of the duellists; it was not the voice of her lover but his rival. Rushing to the window she flung herself to her death. It was the last duel to be fought in Bath, where duelling had always been recognised as a way to settle an argument or quarrel, and duelling was later forbidden throughout England. Both the gaming-room and the room from which the lady committed suicide were long haunted, especially by the sound of clashing swords and the swearing of oaths between the phantom duellists.

The haunting of the Garrick's Head Hotel became more serious than ever when the poltergeist or poltergeists took over. These are the most dangerous of ghosts for they are never seen, and bring terror and fear to any house, inn, or property they may decide to destroy. Evidence of their activities in the hotel bar was documented by a journalist, a Mr Duller of the *Western Daily Press,* who carefully recorded all that he had heard from others and seen for himself during the time of his investigations, reporting them for his paper as late as 1963. A long succession of landlords had been driven out by noises, thumps, bangs; plates and glasses being smashed; cash-machines swept off the counters; bottles bursting in their hands, and disturbed nights of all kinds. One of the landlords had been mystified by a strange and pervasive perfume in the cellar whenever he went down there and he wondered whether the perfume had belonged to the lady who had killed herself. Before the passage had been blocked between the house and the theatre he had often heard the clash of the duellists' swords.

Once, when he heard the sound of footsteps along the secret passage, he sent his son down to confirm what he had heard. His son not only heard the footsteps but saw the figure of a man in Regency costume pass him in the cellar. It is better to quote what Mr Duller himself wrote after deciding to spend a night in the hotel:

> I can vouch for loud and mysterious bumps in the night. It happened when I was staying at the pub two months ago, before I heard the story of the guests. Several thuds woke me as I was dozing in the first floor sitting room. I searched the room and the corridor outside for ten minutes. But I found nothing except that the sounds seemed to have come from the panelling in a corner of the room.

The next morning he told the landlord, who replied:

> I don't believe in ghosts, all the same there's something, some funny things going-on here. Something grips my arms when I'm pouring out drinks for the customers I'm serving at the bar. Something clipped my ear while I was down in the cellar. Something seized my cash-register, weighing half a hundredweight, off the bar and on to a chair, smashing it to pieces.

Is it any wonder then that organised walks take place for tourists to visit the reputed haunted houses of Bath, believers and sceptics alike?

Penfound Manor

CORNWALL

THE DEATH DREAM

One of the most curious of all the many Cornish ghost stories is that of Scorrier House, near Redruth. At that time it belonged to the well-known and extant Williams family, who also own Caerhayes Castle, not a great many miles away. What happened in that house on the night of 11 May 1812 became a matter of national interest when *The Times* newspaper reported it during John Williams' lifetime.

He awoke on that unforgettable night disturbed and frightened by a dream, telling his wife that he had seen a man shot dead in the lobby of the House of Commons, where he had never actually been. The victim of this daylight murder was no less a person than the Chancellor. Every detail in the dream, he told his wife, was crystal clear, so inexplicably clear that he felt nobody would believe it to have been a dream. Mrs Williams, half awake, yet strangely affected by the story, told him it was only a dream and that he would not even remember what he had told her when he woke up next morning, and she turned over to go to sleep again. Some time later, however, her husband again woke her up to tell her that he had had the same dream all over again, the same in every single detail as before.

Mrs Williams, slightly alarmed, again tried to persuade him to go to sleep, assuring him that it was because he had been so concerned by the first dream that it had been repeated. With difficulty she begged him to try once more to go to sleep. Incredible as it seems, John Williams woke his wife for the third time. He insisted that the whole vision of the tragic scene of murder had convinced him that his dream was a reality, for it was impossible that any dream could recur in such detail three times successively.

This time even his wife could say nothing to dissuade him as got up, saw that the time was between one and two o'clock in the morning and dressed himself. At breakfast time he repeated all over again to his wife every single detail of his dream, before leaving for Falmouth, where he had business that day. On his return he said he had told everyone he met about his dream and that no one had a solution to it. The next day they were visited by their daughter and her husband Mr Tucker, who lived in Trematon Castle, one mile south-west of Saltash and one of the most extensive and impressive castles in Cornwall.

Upon the arrival of his son-in-law, John Williams immediately launched into his story of the dream. Mrs Williams laughingly commented to her daughter that he could not even wait to ask Mr Tucker to be seated, so great was his excitement. Upon hearing his father-in-law's obviously phenomenal dream Mr Tucker remarked 'that it might do very well in a dream to have the Chancellor in the lobby of the House of Commons, but that he would never be found there in reality'. He obviously spoke with authority. Mr Tucker then asked him what sort of a person was the victim of the shooting, and after hearing a minutely detailed account of the person by John Williams he remarked: 'Your description is not at all that of the Chancellor, but is certainly that of Mr Spencer Perceval, the Chancellor of the Exchequer; and although he has been to me the greatest enemy I ever met with, for a supposed cause which had no foundation in truth (or words to that effect) I should be exceedingly sorry indeed to hear of his being assassinated, or of any injury of the kind happening to him.'

Mr Tucker then asked him if he had ever seen Mr Spencer Perceval, to which Williams replied that not only had he never seen him but he had also never written to him either concerning private or public matters, nor had any contact with him. What he did know was every detail of the assassin, his face and the clothes he wore at the time, and that the shooting was by a pistol. Furthermore, he added, he had never even been inside the House of Commons or the lobby leading to it. So obsessed was he with his dream that he thought he would depart at once for London to prove that his dream was an absolute reality.

At that very moment a horse was heard galloping up to the house and Mr William's son Michael burst into the room to give them the news of the assassination of the Chancellor of the Exchequer, Mr Spencer Perceval, by a man named Bellingham. He said that he had come as fast as he could from Truro where he had been given the news by a gentleman who had been on the fast mail from London. Michael added that he knew this tragedy would inevitably lead to ministerial confusion, which would affect Mr Tucker politically; the fact that Mr Tucker was already here with the whole family was of great importance, as an immediate journey to London might have to be made.

It was some six weeks later that John Williams himself decided to go to London, expressly to enter the lobby of the House of Commons, to revive the details of his dream in the place where the actual assassination took place. He was accompanied by a friend as a witness of all the details as he had heard them from John Williams. According to the fully authenticated report in a later edition of *The Times* newspaper, from the instant that he entered the lobby everything that he had dreamed returned to him. It was as if he had been there at the very moment Bellingham had entered and fired the shot that killed the Chancellor of the Exchequer. His friend was there beside him to corroborate all his statements, and he proved not only to himself but to his relatives, friends, and all the many other people to whom he had told his story, that it was all true. *The Times* newspaper itself told its readers of this truly amazing story, stating that Mr Williams and many other witnesses were still alive and could have immediately denied the truth of the story, but did not. Furthermore, the editor reported that he had received the whole statement of the case from a correspondent of unquestionable reliability.

THREE RARE GHOSTS

Cornwall has a number of ghost stories and two of the lesser known ones are most unusual. One is of a flute-playing ghost, the other is of a phantom set of teeth. There have been quite a few recorded screaming skulls, two of them in this book, but only one story, so far as can be traced, of teeth that talk. In that remarkably interesting book, *Popular Romances of the West of England*, by R. Hunt, he tells us of the old woman of Perranzabuloe who one day, whilst in the churchyard of St Piran, noticed a strange object on one of the graves which she was greatly surprised to discover was a pair of teeth. Thinking they might well be of great use to her should her own begin to give trouble, she took them up, and put them carefully in her pocket, and on arriving home put them in her bedroom.

To begin with there are close associations between any bones or part of a dead person and the evil practice of black magic, which is still prevalent today in parts of England. The discovery or removal of skulls, bones, or in this case teeth, was usually thought to bring trouble to the remover and was often known to bring a curse upon the person who removed them. It was therefore a great shock to the old woman, when she got into bed, to hear a voice crying out in the bedroom, demanding 'Give me back my teeth.'

She lay immobile and terrified in her bed, for she knew how isolated the village was and remembered stories from her childhood about the most famous of Irish saints, St Piran, who had floated from Ireland to Cornwall on a millstone, on which he had been tied by fanatical heathens some time in the sixth or seventh century. In Perranzabuloe he had built his oratory and stone altar, thus founding his church, the earliest Christianised church in western England, a holy place in the Penhale sands.

She wondered if she had offended the saint in any way. Would she be punished? Should she find St Piran's Well and throw the teeth down it? Was she a thief to take somebody's teeth? Even more frightening, did the teeth belong to the person buried in the grave on which she had found them? Unable to keep them any longer she rose up and threw them out of the window and crept back to her bed. As dawn broke she went downstairs and out into the village to see if the teeth were still there, this time terrified by the sound of running footsteps. But there was not a trace of teeth or footsteps, though the memory of the episode remained with her until she died.

The second Cornish ghost story is only slightly more probable but equally well recorded, and is based on the belief, found across the world, in the ability for human beings to be transformed into animals and resume their own form at will, especially witches who change into cats, black dogs or hares, and earlier still in folklore to wolves, when they were known as were-wolves. Such a transformation was recorded a very long time ago in Looe, where a hare was quite often seen rushing about in the countryside. According to popular belief it had formerly been a village girl who had committed suicide, having been rejected in her love for a sailor. It was noticed soon after her death that whenever misfortune came to Looe she would be seen in the form of a hare rushing down to the Jolly Sailor inn, as if to warn the many people always there. At other times, however, she would play tricks on people and for some inexplicable reason, sportsmen of any kind, particularly huntsmen. This belief in a transformed animal might well have died, but strangely enough some three centuries passed before *Notes and Queries*, 1889, published the following article headed *The Folklore of a Cornish Village*:

> Witches are supposed to have the power of changing their shape and resuming it again at will. A large hare which haunted this neighbourhood had on innumerable occasions baffled the hounds. One luckless day it crossed the path of a party of determined sportsmen who followed it for many miles… with the usual want of success. Before relinquishing the chase one of them who considered the animal to be something beyond an ordinary hare, suggested the trial of silver bullets, and accordingly silver slugs were

beaten into shots for this purpose. The hare was again seen, fired at and this time wounded, though not so effectively as to prevent it running round the brow of the hill and disappearing among the rocks. In searching for the hare they discovered Old Molly crouching under a shelving rock, panting and flushed by the long chase. From that day forward she had a limp in her gait.

Similar cases were notorious in Berkshire and Bolingbroke Castle in Lincolnshire, proving that witches' power is accepted and feared.

The third Cornish ghost story is even more unusual, and is the only example not only in Cornwall but in the whole of Great Britain so far as can be traced in the history of the occult. The story concerns an Elizabethan mansion in Launceston that was not haunted until the early 18th century when the Herle family came to live there. The ghost was a flute-playing spirit, and more intriguing still, it always played an Elizabethan madrigal.

The old Elizabethan mansion that the owner had named Dockacre House had been built on the old road into Launceston and was hidden almost entirely by trees, to maintain complete privacy. It was rumoured to have secret passages running from the cellar to the

Launceston Castle

dominating splendid ruin of Launceston Castle, and to the magnificent church of St Mary Magdalene built by Sir Henry Trecarrel between 1511 and 1524. There had been no signs or mention of hauntings at that time but some time in the year 1714 Nicholas and Elizabeth Herle were living there; on 28 December 1714, Elizabeth was buried in the church and rumours began to circulate that she had been murdered by her husband. The next record one has of Nicholas is that he was a barrister, twice Lord Mayor of Launceston and High Sheriff of Cornwall, known to have been living in Hampstead in London, where he died on 4 August 1728.

It is then that confusion and mystery began, for it was his ghost and not the ghost of Elizabeth who constantly haunted Dockacre House, always playing a flute, and always the same tune. The words of the first verse have been given by James Turner in his excellent book *Ghosts of the South West*:

Since that I saw your Face I resolved
To honour and renown you.
If I be now disdained I wish
My heart had never known you.

Had Nicholas also felt these sentiments when, as was rumoured and never denied, he murdered his wife, either by starving her to death, as one version suggests, or by shooting her on the main staircase? Had Elizabeth become insane towards the end of her life and been shut away and starved, as so often happened in those days, or was she really shot? It was said that there was a permanent bloodstain on the main staircase until the house was altered and restored. And why did Nicholas constantly play his flute whenever he appeared? As so often with ghost stories it is all a great mystery, but that is not the end of the story.

James Turner, who visited the house in the 1960s, said that the owner at that time told him that each successive owner of Dockacre House had passed on a sack of thirteen walking-sticks, one being the strange 'flute-stick'. They seem to be ghosts as well, for unless they are put back in order they all change with each other in an inexplicable supernatural way. As to the 'flute-stick', the owner told him that the flute could no longer be played because it had been blocked up and turned into a walking stick. It all takes a lot of believing, even if you believe in ghosts.

THE MOST EVIL GHOST

Perhaps the most evil Cornish ghost ever recorded in the legends and folklore of the region is that of the corrupt and cruel Bodmin magistrate who was summoned from his grave to be a witness in a most serious case. The charges brought against him were fraud, forgery of documents, illegal possession and sale of lands, and perjury. His name was Jan Tregeagle and his spirit haunts a great number of places in Cornwall, nowhere more than Bodmin Moor, where he is savagely pursued by a band of headless hounds sent by the Devil, to whom he was said to have sold his soul. The roar of savage gales driving across Bodmin Moor on winter nights is even today spoken of as 'the Tregeagle roar.'

He was born in the 1660s somewhere near Bodmin and became a magistrate in spite of his renowned cruelty both to his wife and to his child, with whom he had an incestuous relationship. He became extremely rich and powerful, buying up land wherever he could, either selling it at a huge profit or letting it to tenants at a high rent, greatly feared by the tenants who faced immediate eviction for failure to pay. His notorious conduct in his dealings became known all over Cornwall, especially when it was discovered that before his death Tregeagle, to insure himself against the devil's revenge, had made over a large sum of money to St Breock's Church for masses and prayers to be said for the peace of his soul in eternity. In this he resembled Mephistopheles in Goethe's *Faust,* and after his death and subsequent trial a struggle ensued between Church and Devil for his soul.

The battle was taken up immediately after Tregeagle's death. Almost at once trouble began between tenants and landlords. Discovery of forged documents, disputations over lands sold and resold, and non-payment of rents made court cases mount up between lawyers in all parts of Cornwall. Witnesses were numerous but the whole business of possible settlement became a legal nightmare as the assizes came and went without being able to come to a final judgment. In particular one very large estate claim between landlord and tenant had gone on far too long. The assizes judge was determined to settle the argument satisfactorily and on the day appointed sat in judgment at Bodmin to hear the whole matter. As the day wore on the constant disputes and challenges between prosecution and defence came to a head, and in the late afternoon the judge was suddenly informed that there was yet one more witness who had not been called before. He was therefore ordered by the judge to call him.

At the moment he spoke there was a tremendous clap of thunder that reverberated throughout the whole court, followed by a deep and uneasy silence as the ghost of Tregeagle himself stepped into the witness box before a trembling and white-faced prosecution counsel. The judge, lawyers, witnesses and jury were awe-struck as the ghost confessed to falsity, frauds, forged documents and perjury, enabling the judge to make his brief summing-up to the jury, who returned a verdict of guilty on all charges.

The trial over, the hushed court waited for the sentence to be passed and the prisoner sent to the cells below. It was only by the calm self-possession of the judge that the panic of the crowded court was checked. He quietly requested the defendant to remove the phantom from the witness box and take him back to where he came from. The defendant, after a long pause, gravely told the judge that the ordeal of summoning the spirit from his grave had been so great that he could not undergo the risk of returning him, and he presented the spirit to the court and the church. He then left the court.

The judge decided that the local clergy should be consulted as to what to do with the ghost and he also left the court. The clergy came to the conclusion that since the spirit had made great gifts to them in order that they should protect him by prayers and masses for his soul, they would continue to help him, but they felt that he must also suffer some punishment for all his sins, and that the punishment should be for eternity. So long as he toiled he would preserve his soul from the clutches of the Devil.

The first task the clergy set was the emptying, with a limpet shell, of a bottomless freshwater lake known as Dozmary Pool. This was agreed on by all of them except one, who thought that the task would be harder if the shell was perforated. This suggestion met with approval, and the assignation was carried out at once with the solemn warning that if the spirit ceased to toil the Devil would at once order his Hell Hounds (a pack of headless hounds) to pursue him across the moors until he returned to his task.

According to the theories of the time, Dozmary Pool on Bodmin Moor was believed to be bottomless, one thousand feet above sea-level, one mile in circumference and not fed by any streams. On a clear day it is a lovely sight, but at any other time it is a brooding, uneasy, limitless stretch of water that has never lost its sinister, eerie and even frightening power. It must indeed be menacing when the wild winter gales thrash the water and the moors, haunted to this very day by the ghost of Tregeagle and other ghosts. Most famous among them are those of the dying King Arthur, fatally wounded in the last battle against Mordred, and his faithful knight Sir Bedevere who was commanded by the king to throw his precious sword Escalibur in the lake, where it was seized by a thrice-waving hand and disappeared into the water. Alongside them is the evil spirit of Tregeagle, trying desperately to empty the lake with his perforated limpet shell, while the Hell Hounds wait to pounce on and pursue him when exhausted by his fruitless efforts.

For some time Tregeagle laboured, day after day, week after week, month after month, scooping up water to no avail, making no impression at all. The Devil, meanwhile, was keeping a close watch on his efforts, sending storms, gales, snow and ice to prevent his toils and force him to give in. Robert Hunt in his *Romances of the West of England* has given a graphic account:

> ... lightnings flashed and coiled like fiery snakes around the rocks of Roughtor. Fireballs fell on the desert moors and hissed in the accursed lake. Thunders pealed from the heavens and echoed from hill to hill. An earthquake shook the solid earth and terror was on all living. The winds arose and raged with a fury that was irrestible and hail beat so mercilessly on all things that it spread death around. Long did Tregeagle stand the pelting of the pitiless storm but at length he yielded to its force and fled. The Demons in crowds were at his heels. He doubled however on his pursuers and returned to the lake, but so rapid were they that he could not rest for the required moments to dip the shell in the now seething waters. Three times he fled round the lake and the Evil One pursued him. Then feeling that there was no safety for him near Dozmary Pool he sprang swifter than the wind across it shrieking with agony, and thus since the Devils cannot cross water and were obliged to go round the lake he gained on them and fled over the moor, and did not sleep a wink that night...

He ran until he reached the chapel of Roche Rock (though another legend says St Breock, where he was buried), his screams heard for miles round until on thrusting his head through the east window to try and gain sanctuary he finally fell silent. But only his head reached through the window; the rest of his body was exposed to the raging gale and the howling of the Hell Hounds waiting for him.

In fear and desperation Tregeagle prayed and called upon St

Petroc to help him, and the saint protected him and guided him to Padstow Beach (St Petroc being the saint of Padstow). There the church took up its interrupted task of punishment, commanding him to weave ropes of sand from the beach and forcing him to go on weaving until the tides swept in and washed the ropes away. His howls of rage and disappointment caused so much anger in the town of Padstow that local people, by their protests, forced him to move yet again. This he did with the help of the saint, who binding him in one of his ropes of sand bore him to Berepper, near Helston, where he set him another task.

> This time he was commanded to carry sacks of sand across the Loe estuary and empty them in Porthleven. It was then that one of the Demons acted, for as Tregeagle laboriously carried his heavy sacks across the estuary the Demon tripped him up, thus spilling all his sand, which became a ridge known to this day as Loe Bar. This made the people of Helston and the neighbourhood very angry and caused more protests. Yet again, and this for the last time, though unknown to Tregeagle, the Church ordered him to be sent to the Lands End at Porthcurno Cove from which he was to sweep the sands into Mill Bay. Tregeagle is still said to have been seen long ago in his labours, battling with the fierce Atlantic waves as they washed the sand away. Legend seems to offer no explanation for the disappearance of his ghost, but even today, when the bad winter gales wreak havoc, it is claimed that Tregeagle's howls and screams can be heard above the roar of the winds.

Surely the greatest challenge to any disbeliever in the supernatural would be to find himself or herself alone on Bodmin Moor, near Loe Bar or in Porthcurno Cove in a howling Atlantic gale and not have any fear. But it might be thought that Tregeagle had given in after all under the terrible punishments imposed by the Church, and his soul been claimed and held by the Devil and his Hell Hounds at last.

THE HAUNTED CHURCH AND MANOR HOUSE

It is rare indeed to find two ghosts of one family haunting the manor they lived in and the church of which they held the living. Yet in the parish of Poundstock both church and manor were haunted by two members of the ancient family of the Penfounds. The first haunting had its origins in the 14th century, the second in the 17th century, and even in recent times both apparitions have been seen. The church of St Neot, Poundstock, was the scene of dramatic and horrifying events when in December 1356 the curate William Penfound was brutally murdered after celebrating Mass. One year later Bishop Grandison of Exeter recorded a full account, as follows:

> Certain satellites of Satan, names unknown, on the Feast of St John the Apostle – which makes the crime worse – broke into the Parish Church of Poundstock within our Diocese with a host of armed men, during Mass, and before Mass was scarcely completed they furiously entered the Chancel and with swords and staves cut down William Penfound, clerk. Vestments and other Church Ornaments were desecrated with human blood in contempt of the Creator, in contempt of the Church, to the subversion of ecclesiastical liberty and the disturbance of the peace of the realm. Where will we be safe from crime if the Holy Church, our Mother, the House of God and the Gateway to Heaven is thus deprived of its sanctity?

Later still, on 13 February 1358, a document in the Patent Roll of Edward III (1327–1377) commands three men to 'make inquisition in the county of Cornwall touching all persons concerned in the death of William Penfound killed in Poundstock Church, and to take and imprison in Launceston Gaol all persons indicted of the felony.' No reason has ever been given for the murder. However, two ringleaders of the crime were later named as John Bovill and Simon de St Gennys who were arrested but at their trial pardoned, no doubt claiming 'benefit of clergy', which would make them immune to any sentence passed in a secular court. At that time the Lollards, under Wycliffe, were preaching all over Cornwall against the corrupt clergy, and it was not impossible to believe that the murderers of William Penfound were Lollards. Whoever they were, the ghost of William Penfound was said to have been seen from that very day, wandering in and out of the church and round the cemetery and even as far as the manor in which the family continued to live for another four centuries.

The Penfounds were a remarkable family who claimed their descent from a Saxon named Briend, a tenant of the land on which the present manor was built, his landlord being Edith, wife of Edward the Confessor, as recorded in the Domesday Book. The earliest documentary evidence to date the building of Penfound Manor is from the 14th century some time before William Penfound's murder in 1356, and it is one of the oldest inhabited manors in England. It was alienated under a decree of Chancery in 1759 by Ambrose Penfound. The last of the Penfounds in the direct line was Henry Pollexfen Penfound, born in 1761, who died in 1847, aged 86, in the 'Poor House' of Poundstock 'leaving issue in a state of poverty'.

The house was built round the medieval Great Hall, which originally had a rush-strewn earth floor in the centre of which the fire was placed. The smoke then had no method of escape and later the fireplace was built, which still remains. The first addition was the Norman wing built on to the Great Hall, consisting of the Ladies' Bower and the single bedroom known as the Solar. The Solar was its first bedroom and later became widely known as the Haunted Room. It remained the only bedroom until 1589, when the staircase known also as the Haunted Staircase was built, and a second bedroom was built over the Buttery. Coming to the manor through the tall, iron, Florentine gates leading to the courtyard is like entering straight into its history. It is closely connected with another fine house called Trebarfoot Manor through the link between the Penfound and the Trebarfoot families, first as close friends, then as bitter enemies, and is haunted even today by the ghost of Kate Penfound.

The Penfounds were never knighted or ennobled but were respected and feared as rich and powerful landed gentry. They were rebels; devout Roman Catholics and prepared to die for their faith. They were Royalists, fine swordsmen, quarrelsome, constantly issuing and receiving writs over land and property and not averse to smuggling; although not actual smugglers themselves they had a long cellar near Bude, an area rife with smugglers and with easy access to Cornish coves and beaches.

The Civil Wars soon brought tragedy to the family when on 16 May, 1643, in the battle of Stratton, one of the Penfounds was killed. They had come out for the King; their neighbours and friends, the Trebarfoots, were for Cromwell. Some time before that, however, trouble had been brewing between them when both families learned that Kate Penfound was deeply in love with John Trebarfoot. In those times the Stuart families exercised their medieval right to select husbands for their daughters, irrespective of their ages and without giving them the chance to meet the men they were to marry. They could be bought into convents by generous money gifts to the Abbots or Abbesses, or sold in marriage to another family.

Penfound Manor

Serious attempts were obviously being made by Kate's father to forbid Kate even seeing John Trebarfoot, but the two had plans for an elopement, which was then fashionable. The date was set by the two of them for April 26, when they were to meet at 'midnight sharp'. No year is given in any of the documents available, but it might well have been around the time Kate's grandfather was killed in the battle of Stratton. There are various versions of what happened. Kate was then sleeping in the Solar, her parents in the second bedroom. When she had assured herself that her parents were fast asleep, Kate climbed through the Solar window and descended to the courtyard down a ladder John Trebarfoot had placed for her. His horse stood tethered, and the gates wide open for an immediate escape. Another version says that Kate used the staircase to go down to meet her lover. One accurate account of everything the Penfounds did during their four centuries of ownership has been given in a little book entitled *Penfound Manor*. The authors were Mr and Mrs Tucker who were tenants there for some time in the 1960s and had access to a great number of documents in the Public Record Office in London and the reference library of Truro. They state that Arthur Penfound, Kate's father, was not asleep but was enjoying a glass of grog before retiring, and hearing the noise of Kate descending the ladder, immediately rushed down the staircase into the courtyard with his sword already.

Accounts of what happened next diverge. One says that he first killed John Trebarfoot and then his own daughter, which seems improbable. Another account suggests that he rushed at Trebarfoot accidentally killing his daughter who had rushed to interpose the two men. Yet another states that a duel took place between the two men in which both died. Whatever the truth of the matter, the ghost of Kate Penfound has become a legend, and April 26 is said to be powerfully remembered every year in the village of Poundstock and beyond. During the time they lived in Penfound, Kenneth and Doris Tucker wrote the following words regarding the ghost of Kate:

> Whilst we have neither seen nor heard anything strange or odd, it is only fair to say that we have had contact, both personal and by correspondence, with many people who have told us of their experiences of supernatural manifestations here, including in two cases the actual sight of Kate. These have seemed to us to be quite normal people, with no particular interest in psychic matters, and we remain open-minded and very ready to welcome all three ghosts should they favour us with a visit.

There could be no better ending to a ghost story than these generous words. The Tuckers' stay in the manor must in itself have left them with lasting memories, and in a few heart-felt words they describe: '…the indescribable atmosphere of serenity, tranquillity and peace which pervades every room, every vista, almost every stone.' It is a great pity that Penfound Manor, set on a hill above fields sloping to the valley of the little river Bude, and surrounded completely by its medieval wall, is no longer open to the public.

THE TORMENTED SPIRIT

In the invaluable *Historical Survey of the County of Cornwall*, published in 1817, there is authentically recorded one of the most astonishing ghost stories not only in Cornwall but in the United Kingdom. It was meticulously detailed and written down by the person who undertook not only to see and meet the ghost, but to carry out the exorcism that would bring it peace and freedom. Even to those people, and there are a great number of them, who believe in ghosts and the supernatural, this mysterious story will perhaps be hard to accept, though the truth of it all is quite evident. It was recorded by the Reverend John Ruddle, Vicar of Altarnun, incumbent of Launceston and later Prebendary of Exeter Cathedral.

The story began on 20 June 1665, when Ruddle conducted a funeral service in South Petherton church, at the end of which he was implored by a most distressed mourner to come and visit him as soon as possible. It was then Thursday, and Ruddle regretted that he could not manage a visit before Monday, which seemed only to increase the elderly man's distress. He gave his name as Bligh, a farmer, of nearby Botathan House. Such was his anxiety that he even sent a messenger on Sunday, repeating his request, so that when Ruddle arrived on Monday lunchtime he was more than surprised to find another minister already there. Mrs Bligh seemed impatient and distressed, even more so than her husband, though they all sat down to lunch without any reference to the reason for Ruddle's visit. It was not until after lunch that the minister suggested to Ruddle that they should walk in the garden, where he informed Ruddle of what was happening in the Bligh family. Their son Sam was causing severe concern to his parents with his constant fear of a female ghost which was frightening the boy so much that he would no longer cross the fields to reach his school. The minister then requested that as he himself knew nothing about ghosts, even if there were such things, would Ruddle see what he could do to help them, to which Ruddle, after a long pause, agreed.

Upon returning to the house Ruddle said he would like to see their son Sam and was led by Mrs Bligh to the orchard where the boy was sitting. She then left them. Without even a word to Ruddle the boy burst into tears. Then he told him that his parents were unkind to him, they thought he was a liar, they laughed at him, said he was trying to dodge school, had fallen in love with a girl, and that there was no such thing as the ghost that he believed he had seen. They said that he was a liar to say that he had seen her, not just once, but every time he crossed the field, called Higher Brown Quartils.

Then suddenly he began crying again and Ruddle knew for certain that the boy was speaking the truth. After a few moments he asked the boy to tell him everything that was troubling him. Interrupted by tears, his story gave Ruddle the full details of his problem. The woman who appeared to him had been a neighbour of his father and had died about eight years ago. Her name was Dorothy Dingley. She never spoke to him but passed by him hastily and always left the footpath to him. She commonly met him twice or three times in the breadth of the field.

It was about two months before he took notice of her, and though her face was in his memory he did not recall her name but supposed her to be some woman who lived somewhere nearby, because he had seen her there on frequent occasions. He did not imagine anything to the contrary until she began to meet him constantly, morning and evening, and always in the Higher Brown Quartils field, sometimes two or three times in the breadth of it as he had described.

The first time he took notice of her was about a year ago when he began to suspect her of being a ghost. He had courage enough not to be afraid and kept the secret to himself for a good while, though very much puzzled about it. He often spoke to the woman but never had a word in answer. Then he decided to change his way and went to school by the Under House Road. She then began to meet him in the narrow lane between the Quarry Park and the Nursery, which was worse. At length he began to be terrified of her and prayed continually that God would either free him from the ordeal or let him know the meaning of it all.

Night and day, sleeping or waking, her face was constantly in his mind, and he grew so pensive that it was noticed by all the family. He told his brother William about it and later even his father and mother, who kept it to themselves for some time before they began to start their taunting, telling him to continue to go to school whatever happened, and put such fripperies out of his mind. But always the woman was waiting for him.

The boy then stopped and in the silence Ruddle, deeply impressed by the boy's sincerity and truthfulness, decided to do everything in his power to help him, and told the boy so. 'Thank God,' said the boy, 'Now I shall at least be believed.' Ruddle then told him to meet him the next day at six o'clock in the morning to see if the ghost would be there. He was to say nothing to anyone, not even his parents, until the time to do so was right. They at once returned to the house where Mr and Mrs Bligh and the minister hurried to meet them, expectant and eager to hear what had happened. Ruddle simply said he had promised to help the boy in every possible way, that he implicitly believed what Sam had told him and that he would do everything in his power to fulfil his promise, and he begged them to have confidence in him.

Meanwhile he met Sam, as promised, in the field the next morning. Part way across the ghost appeared, exactly as Sam had described, and passed them by. Ruddle had intended to speak to the spectre but found he had no power to do so, though he was careful not to show his fear to Sam. He promised the family that he would return as soon as possible, adding that as he had a number of parochial duties to carry out he could not say exactly when he would return, but it would be as soon as he could do so, though he was aware that they did not seem to be fully satisfied.

Largely owing to the fact that his wife became very ill it was in fact three weeks before Ruddle came again to the house. As he could not forget the boy's state of mind about the ghost, his first duty had been to obtain permission from the Bishop of Exeter to perform the ceremony of exorcism if, as he himself thought, it was the only way to give peace to the ghost. He also had a collection of books on the supernatural, regarded in those days as the Power of Darkness and the work of the Devil, to combat which great faith in God was required. He would also carry a crucifix with him in anything he would have to do. He wondered too about Dorothy Dingley, who she was and why she was haunting the boy. Had she or someone connected with her committed a crime? Finally the day arrived when he was able to resume his contact with the spirit. It was 27 July 1665 when he decided to search the fields once again for the ghost. It was very early in the morning that he set out to find her before going to the house. He wrote every detail of this visit down in his journal as follows:

> I went to the haunted field by myself, and walked the breadth of the field without any encounter. I returned and took the other walk, and then the spectrum appeared to me at much about the same place where I saw it before, when the young gentleman was with me. In my thoughts it moved swifter than the time before, and about ten feet distant from me on my right hand, insomuch that I had not time to speak, as I had determined with myself beforehand.

He then went to the house to explain to the family what he had seen and to prove the truth of the boy's statements, and implored the father and mother to go with him and their son early the next morning and see for themselves. They were most uneasy, but agreed, saying they would leave at five o'clock in the morning and tell the servants they had work to do in the fields. Ruddle writes again:

> ...I took my horse and fetched a compass another way and so met them at the stile we had appointed. Thence we all four walked leisurely in the Quartils, and had passed above half the field before the ghost made appearance. It then came over the stile just

before us, and moved with that swiftness that by the time we had gone six or seven steps it passed by. I immediately turned my head and ran after it, with the young man by my side; we saw it pass over the stile by which we entered, but no farther. I stepped upon the hedge at one place, he at another, but could discern nothing; whereas I dare aver that the swiftest horse in England could not have conveyed himself out of sight in that short space of time. Two things I observed in this day's appearance: (1) That a spaniel dog, who followed the company unregarded, did bark and run away as the spectrum passed by; whence it is easy to conclude that it was not our fear or fancy which made the apparition; (2) That the motion of the spectrum was not by steps and moving of the feet, but a kind of gliding, as children upon ice or a boat down a swift river.

The family were terrified at what they had witnessed, for they had seen the Dorothy Dingley whose funeral they had attended eight years before, and whose death had been suspicious. Had she been given a child by Sam's brother, who had suddenly gone to London and never returned? Had one or other murdered the babe? Rumours there had been, and they were still strong after all these years. When Ruddle asked the family if they would repeat the expedition again they categorically refused, saying that they would leave everything to him, but they acknowledged that Sam had told the truth.

Ruddle was completely convinced that he had work to do in order to give comfort and quiet to this tormented ghost whose crime, if such it were, had caused her repeated appearances to Sam Bligh. There was no other possible solution to the problem, only exorcism, ministered by a priest who believed deeply in his task, and this as soon as it could be done. In those days witches and ghosts were supposed to be unable to exercise their spells on anyone who had said three masses beforehand, carried a crucifix and held a rowan stick in their hand as protection. Ruddle would have known of such things from his books, but his own account of what he did on that wonderful morning is one of the most remarkable ghost stories to be found in our language:

The next morning being Thursday, I went out very early by myself, and walked for about an hour's space in meditation and prayer, in the field next adjoining to the Quartiles; soon after five, I stepped over the stile in to the disturbed field, and had not gone above thirty or forty paces, before the ghost appeared at the farther stile, I spoke to it with a loud voice, in some such sentences, as the way of these dealings directed me, whereupon it approached, but slowly, and when I came near, it moved not, I spoke again, and it answered in a voice neither very audible nor intelligible; I was not the least terrified, and therefore persisted, until it spake again and gave me satisfaction, but the work could not be finished at this time, wherefore the same evening, an hour after sunset it met me again, near the same place, and after a few words of each side, it quietly vanished, and neither doth appear since nor ever will more to any man's disturbance, the discourse in the morning lasted about a quarter of an hour.

These things are true and I know them to be so, with as much certainty as eyes and ears can give me, and until I can be persuaded that my senses do deceive me about their proper objects, and by that persuasion deprive myself of the strongest inducement to believe the Christian religion, I must and will assert these things in this paper are true, and for the manner of my proceeding I find no reason to be ashamed of, for I can justify it to men of good principles, discretion, and recondite learning, though in this case I choose to content myself in the assurance of the thing, rather than be at the unprofitable trouble to persuade others to believe, for I know full well with what difficulty relations of so uncommon a nature and practice obtain belief.

To the ignorance of men in our age in this peculiar, and mysterious part of philosophy and religion, namely, the communication between spirits and men, not one scholar out of ten thousand though otherwise of excellent learning knows any thing of it, or the way how to manage it; this ignorance breeds fear and abhorrence of that, which otherwise might be of incomparable benefit to mankind.

THE BODMIN MOOR GHOST

More than one hundred years ago a visitor to Cornwall had been fishing in one of the streams on Bodmin Moor. It was evening when he decided it was time to go home for he had heard more than once from local people that the moor was no place to be at night. He was about to step across a stream when suddenly a figure appeared from nowhere. It was a young girl who wore a silk bonnet, a coloured gown and a red shawl. She was walking carefully, picking her way over the marshy ground then stopping to gaze across the moor, as if expecting someone or something, before moving again. As he called out 'Good night' she vanished. When he returned to the house where he was a guest he told his host what had happened to him, puzzled and not a little afraid at what he had seen. His host gravely told him he had seen the ghost of a young girl named Charlotte Dymond, who had been murdered at the spot where his guest had seen her, and that nearby was a stone monument to her memory. He repeated by heart the words engraved thereon: 'Monument erected by private subscription in memory of Charlotte Dymond, who was murdered by Matthew Weeks, Sunday April 14th, 1844.'

Since her death her ghost had been seen by many people but none recently, so this story would make good local news if it was reported to the local newspaper. He himself never had, nor wished to see it; there were dangers enough on Bodmin Moor by night and day, especially in bad weather.

Charlotte Dymond had been a dairymaid at Lower Penhale Farm, belonging to a widow named Philippa Peter, in the parish of the nearby hamlet of Davidstow. It was a hard-working farm, for the winters could be harsh, the peat bogs were never easy to dig at any time and the land was poor. Whenever it snowed, as it did so often, the farm was completely cut off, and even in the summer it could only be reached by rough tracks. Mrs Peter was a happy and a hard-working woman, loved by her son John, Charlotte who was her dairymaid, her servant John Stevens, and her general labourer Matthew Weeks. Not one of them could ever have imagined the impending tragedy, which was to bring endless grief to them and to the whole neighbourhood.

If anything worried Mrs Peter it was Matthew Weeks, who was rough and made extremely jealous by Charlotte's behaviour, with her taunting and playful boasting of flirtations with the village boys. Not only were the other boys younger, but they were also more active

Bodmin Moor

than Matthew, who limped and was conscious of his disablement. On Sundays especially he showed his jealous anger, for she wore all her best clothes to go to chapel and meet the other boys, with whom she would laugh, joke and flirt while he would either go for a walk alone or remain round the farm.

The Sunday outings could only take place, however, in the spring and summer. Often for weeks during the winter months they could go nowhere and had to make the best of Sundays by playing games or charades, reading, or singing round the piano, with Mrs Peter playing. Immediately spring came they were free to go out, and Charlotte would put on her 'courting clothes', as she called them, to go off to chapel. Mrs Peter then became worried at the change in Matthew's character, for he was paying far more attention than she liked to Charlotte, who seemed to enjoy teasing him and often caused quarrels, though they were soon healed.

It was on Sunday, 14 April 1844, that something occurred on the farm which prevented Charlotte from going to chapel, giving Matthew the opportunity he so badly needed to persuade her to go for a walk with him after lunch, to which she could only agree, since she had no other excuse. For her part Mrs Peter was only too pleased, for they both laughed and joked together. It was a beautiful spring day when they set out at 4 o'clock in the afternoon, intending to be back in time for Charlotte to go to chapel for the evening service. Matthew had already decided that they would go to Lanlavery Rock and on to the far slopes of Roughtor, and down the long road leading to Camelford.

She was looking particularly beautiful and flirtatious in her Sunday 'courting clothes' which she kept in a trunk all the rest of the week. Matthew knew about this, since he had often looked into it, lovingly touching each garment. Today she was wearing 'a gown of different colours, partly green, a red cloth shawl, a black silk bonnet, and a black silk handbag trimmed with black silk trimmings which she carried on her arm. The ribbons on her bonnet were light in colour and she had on a pair of pattens.' She also wore her favourite bead necklace and carried her gloves. This was too much for his jealousy. He feared that such clothes were fit only for attracting other young men who were not lame as he was and not dressed in such worn and shabby clothes. What Charlotte Dymond did not know, and could never have dreamed of, was that Matthew Weeks had a knife concealed in his pocket, and in his heart a fierce jealousy that if she would not have him he would never let her have any other man. Life on a moor farm was hard enough, and there was not much fun to be had outside. The teasing between them suddenly turned sour when she taunted Matthew with the name Tommy Prout, whom she liked very much and who she felt liked her. They had reached a gate leading into a field, Higher Downgate, when he suddenly caught hold of her. What happened then is best described in the words of his own confession at his subsequent trial for murder:

> I told her I had seen her in a situation with some young man that was disgraceful to her. She then said: 'I shall do as I like. I shall have nothing more to do with you.' I took out my knife and then replaced it. But on her repeating the phrase, I made a cut at her throat from behind. She immediately fell backwards, the blood gushing out in a large stream and exclaimed while falling, 'Lord have mercy on me.' While she was on the ground I made a second but much larger cut though she was almost dead at the time. After standing over her body about four or five minutes, I lifted up one of her arms and it fell to the ground as if she was dead. I then pushed her body a little further down the bank. I afterwards took her bonnet, shawl, shoes and pattens and covered them up in a turf pit. Her gloves and bag I put into my pocket. In the road I threw away the knife.

At the farm an anxious Mrs Peter, with her son and Stevens, were wondering why the two had not yet returned. Her anxiety increased to real fear when Matthew Weeks came back alone with an explanation that he had left Charlotte at the cottage of a Mr Spear, near Brown Willy (the only mountain in Cornwall), because Charlotte was not happy with Mrs Peter and Mr Spear had promised to find her a new job in the village of Blisland.

To Mrs Peter the story did not seem at all likely, because Charlotte had told her over and over again how happy she was on the farm. Mrs Peter had also been more than aware of Matthew Weeks' jealousy concerning Charlotte's activities. She may well have gone herself to Mr Spear's cottage the next day and learned that Charlotte had never been there on the Sunday, when he himself had been at home all day. She said nothing to Matthew Weeks, but told the police that Charlotte was now missing from the farm and explained her fears. At once an immense and thorough search was made of Bodmin Moor. Meanwhile Matthew Weeks had disappeared. Thomas Rickard, a constable from Davidstow, was the man who found Charlotte's dead body at last, almost at the end of April, cunningly disposed of by Matthew Weeks as described at his trial. According to the evidence of the Constable:

> She was lying in a wild and desolate spot, rarely trodden by the foot of man and with no human habitation near it, in a water course. I took possession of her shoes, her bonnet, and her whiff with a piece of string attached.

Thomas Good, a surgeon living at Lewannick, saw at once that the body had no self-inflicted wound but had clearly been murdered. He himself, together with a small party that had already gathered there, laid the body on a hurdle and with great difficulty bore it slowly over the deep and marshy land that lay all around the stream. Carefully they brought the body back to Lower Penhale Farm where Mrs Peter, her son John, and Stevens her servant were waiting in a stunned silence. There Dr Good made a final full examination, telling Mrs Peter that the body was young and healthy, that there was no sign of a pregnancy nor of any violation other than the cut throat. The hunt for the murderer ended a few days later when Matthew Weeks was found on Plymouth Hoe, having tried to escape by boat, and arrested. His trial was fixed for 9 August 1844 at Bodmin assizes.

The *Royal Cornwall Gazette* gave the following report:

> The prisoner is about 5'4" high and lame. He has a good head of hair of brownish colour and curly; his eyes are what is commonly called down looking, the eyebrows overhung, and he is slightly marked with a smallpox. Dressed in a blue cloth shooting jacket, a black stock ornamented with a pin; a fancy waistcoat with three rows of glass buttons and a pair of greyish trowsers.

The concern about this young girl's brutal murder spread all over Cornwall, but it was most deeply felt locally, particularly by Mrs Peter who had suffered a great loss, for they had been extremely fond of each other. After the post-mortem Charlotte Dymond's body was laid to rest in Davidstow Churchyard, between three of the Peters graves. Some unknown person affectionately laid a stone cross above the small grave.

On 12 August 1844 Matthew Weeks was tried, condemned to death for murdering Charlotte Dymond and hanged on the same day. According to the account book of the assize court the executioner was George Mitchell, who 'was not allowed his salary until the summer assize when he was paid £25 for carrying out his duties'.

Shortly after this a stone monument was erected on the spot at which Charlotte Dymond's body had been found at the foot of Roughtor. It was paid for by hundreds of local people as a token of their sorrow and grief and the simple words incised upon it read:

> MONUMENT ERECTED BY
> PRIVATE SUBSCRIPTION
> IN MEMORY OF
> CHARLOTTE DYMOND
> WHO WAS MURDERED BY
> MATTHEW WEEKS
>
> SUNDAY APRIL 14th 1844

The hauntings began everywhere round the spot, at her grave in the churchyard and round Lower Penhale Farm. Only the morbid would try to see it in daylight and no-one would dare to be on Bodmin Moor at night unless they had been lost while out walking. The writer, James Turner, when researching for the story around the 1970s, spoke to a farmer whose father and mother had taken over Lower Penhale Farm after the death of Mrs Peter. He said that his mother often spoke of Charlotte Dymond and owned a scent bottle which she said was found clutched in Charlotte's hand. She had been told that they had warned the girl not to go out on the moor, even on the very day she was murdered. Was this scent bottle one of the articles Constable Rickard 'took possession of' when he discovered the body, describing it as 'a whiff with a piece of string attached'?

Bodmin Moor has claimed many lives in past centuries but perhaps none so young and innocent as Charlotte Dymond.

Lew Trenchard

DEVON

THE SINISTER SECRET ROOM

Among the numerous haunted houses of England there have been a number with secret rooms, but none more sinister and terrifying than that of Chambercombe Manor, 1 mile south-east of Ilfracombe. The manor is secluded in a deep valley running down to the sea, a valley well frequented by smugglers in the heyday of smuggling between 1750 and 1850, when a tunnel ran under the splendid cobbled courtyard of the manor. From a distance one can see the outside of the secret room. Many distinguished aristocratic families possessed the house from the 12th century, and their most distinguished guest was Lady Jane Grey, before she became the queen who ruled for only nine days and was executed, in 1553. The room in which she slept is called the Lady Jane Grey Room.

Towards the end of the 16th century the Gorges family sold all their lands and gave the title deeds to the vicar of Ilfracombe as trustee, who split up the lands into small parcels known as 'ropers' and rented them to various farmers. In 1885 it was one of these farmers who discovered the secret room quite by chance. He had been pestered continually by his wife to do something about a leaking roof, so one day when she was away visiting the market and would be absent for some time, he took a long ladder and went up to inspect the roof. While he was climbing up he noticed with astonishment what looked like the outline of a window belonging to a room he had never seen, though he had lived in the manor farm for some years. He at once began investigating the brickwork surrounding the outline of the window. He then made a hole large enough for him to see a dark interior that might at one time have been a store-room.

He came down the ladder and went into the house and up the stairs to see if there were any trace of a room. He noticed unusual markings on the wall between the Lady Jane Room and the next room, the Victorian Room as it was later called, so faint that neither he nor his wife had ever noticed them. He next fetched a pickaxe and discovered a solid wall that finally yielded to his heavy blows. Continuing with now mounting excitement, thinking there might be hidden treasure to be found, he worked faster. Like all the previous tenants, he had always known the manor to be haunted, but that there was a secret passage or tunnel, he did not know. There had been nights when they were frightened by the sound of barrels being rolled along, having been brought up from the beach. Some had actually seen the smuggling and the smugglers themselves but had learned that they must keep their mouths shut if they were to have their own share of brandy, gin and wine. So it was more than probable that he had discovered something connected with that. Encouraged by the idea of what might be hidden in what he was sure was a secret room, he had made a hole large enough to look through when his wife suddenly appeared back from the market. Her curiosity overcoming her anger at the mess everywhere, she watched him continue until he had made an aperture large enough for his body to pass through.

He told his wife to go and fetch some candles, for it was pitch dark inside, oppressive and smelling of damp and decay. At last, holding their lighted candles, first he and then his wife wormed their way through the wall, stunned by what they saw. The light from the flickering candles revealed a long, narrow, low-ceilinged room; the tattered shreds of what might once have been tapestry hung from the walls. There was a wardrobe, a table and chairs, all rotting away with damp and age. The whole centre of the room was occupied by a magnificent four-poster bed. The once-splendid hangings were shrouded with dense cobwebs, as was the whole room, which reeked of damp and rot.

Thick dust covered the floor so that the two made no sound as they moved apprehensively toward the bed, fearful of what was behind the hangings that enclosed it. A very thin light filtered through the enclosed window frame the farmer had first discovered. Eventually, urged on by his wife, who dared not move, the farmer edged forward and as he slowly drew apart the heavy bed hangings a hideous shriek from his wife cut into the silence. There on a pillow, yellow with age, lay a grinning skull; on the faded crimson coverlet lay a skeletal arm and fingers tightly clutching the linen sheet; the rest of the skeleton lay hidden under the coverlet. The terrible silence was broken as the farmer's wife crashed heavily to the floor in a dead faint. He turned to revive her so that both of them could escape from the terrible room, for what they had witnessed was unforgettable.

Later on, when they had started to recover from the shock of what they had seen, they both knew that the first thing they must do was to replace the part of the wall that had been broken into; the work would have to be done by the farmer without the help of the farmhands. When that was done they would give notice, quit the farm and never come back. Neither of them could have known that the secret room and its contents were to become one of the outstanding mysteries of Devonshire folklore. The story became known as the legend of Kate Oatway, daughter of William and Ellen Oatway.

William's father was Alexander Oatway, a renowned smuggler and wrecker of Ilfracombe, who had rented Chambercombe Manor from the Vicar of Ilfracombe in a parcel of land known as a roper. One story says that it was Alexander Oatway who lured a ship on to the rocks by false lantern signals, found one of the survivors, who was thought to be a titled and wealthy Spanish lady, and brought her up the secret passage to the manor farm, where he robbed her. To avoid any suspicion he walled her up in the secret room and left her to die of starvation.

Another version of the story says that it was not Alexander but his son William who carried out the murder. After his father's death William took over Chambercombe Farm, which with its secret passage and his own personal skill at wrecking and smuggling suited him admirably.

One night there was a terrible storm that drove a ship onto the rocks. It was not long before William went down to the sea, certain there would be plunder to be had from any survivors. He soon saw that one survivor was lying on the rocks having been flung out of the stricken ship. His lantern showed him the sodden body of a woman, obviously unconscious, her head and face covered with blood. As he bent over to examine the body more closely, his sharp eyes saw that she was richly dressed, with flashing diamonds on two of her fingers and a small leather case clutched in one hand. He was a very strong man and was able to lift the body and carry it through the secret passage and into the house, where Ellen his wife was anxiously waiting for him. As he carefully placed the body on a couch for Ellen to attend to, his wife started. Her quick eyes noticed the diamonds and other jewels, but it was what she saw in the remains of the damaged face that alarmed her.

William again lifted the body and took it upstairs to a small room next to the Lady Jane Grey Room, where he left her to change his clothes and tell Ellen to undress and wash the body. When he returned he saw that Ellen had done what he asked, and the woman was lying in the huge four-poster bed of the richly furnished room. On a table beside the bed Ellen had put the diamond rings, necklace, earrings and other pieces of jewellery. Turning to her husband she told him that what was left of the woman's face closely resembled their daughter Kate, and she pointed to a piece of jewellery stamped with the letter W, which she said she had given Kate when she was quite young on her engagement to a rich young Irishman named Wallis.

Early the next morning a young man named Roley, who had been watching the wreck, called to ask William if he had managed to save a survivor from drowning as he had seen him lift something heavy and carry it off the rocks. In spite of his denial William saw that the young man remained unconvinced, though he apologised for disturbing him and making such a mistake.

A few days later another, and totally unexpected visitor came to the farm, quietly announcing that he was the skipper of the wrecked ship. He said that of his crew, one of his sailors as well as his first mate had been saved from drowning, but that one of his passengers, a most important lady, had been thrown on to the rocks and might well have survived. Someone had told him that he, Mr Oatway, had been seen carrying a very heavy burden away from the rocks. He asked if perhaps it was the lady who had survived. Oatway asked him who she was, this important lady.

The skipper told him she was a lady from the north of Ireland travelling to Bristol. She seemed to know the coast very well, as if she had lived in Ilfracombe or nearby at some time. Her name was Wallis, a very rich lady he understood from what she told him. William nodded but said he had no knowledge of such a lady, nor had he carried her to his farm as the skipper had been informed. The skipper turned to leave, but like the previous visitor, William saw that he was totally unconvinced.

Almost as soon as he had departed William and Ellen decided they must seal the room up and leave as soon as possible. The diamonds and jewels would help them to make a new future. William's reputation was fairly well known, he had enemies and quite a few unpaid debts to local people. That night they left the district. Legends conflict as to how they ended, but one reports that Ellen died soon after and that William lived to the age of 79, when he died in a cottage, but it does not say where. Before his death he had written out a confession of his crime, which was found hidden behind the fireplace when the cottage was undergoing repairs.

Chambercombe Manor is privately owned and open to the public. The interior of the secret room may be seen on the guided tour of the manor. It is visible through a small glass pane and sadly has little interest except to the very curious. Its tragedy lives on in the minds of those who read and love folklore and legends.

THE VISITATION OF 'OLD MADAM'

Madam Gould died in her favourite straight-backed chair on 10 April 1795. Almost immediately all the shutters of her farm-house flew open of themselves, and one of the farm-hands working in a field, disturbed by the crash of wood against walls, hurried to the house to see what had happened. On his way he saw his mistress standing under a walnut tree. He had no idea what had happened until he was told she was dead, when he realised he must have seen her ghost. It was, in fact, the first of many appearances in and about Lew Trenchard in Devon.

This determined and single-minded woman, known everywhere as Old Madam, had been widowed by the death of her husband in 1766 and left with a son David and a daughter Margaret. Her son squandered almost all his inheritance so that Old Madam was forced to recover what she could of the estate, and set about doing so, taking over farm after farm and running them herself. Her strong and

'Old Madam'

fearless character overcame every obstacle until she had achieved what she had set out to do.

Seven days after her funeral – which her son-in-law had refused to attend because she had once told him she had cut him out of her will – she made her second appearance, an astounding one indeed to the man who saw her. He had left Lew Trenchard many years before to go to America and had now returned and was living nearby. He had hired a horse at Tavistock to ride to Galford, where he spent the day and evening, so that he was on his way back as the moon shone over the countryside.

He was suddenly startled by the sight of a lady in a white satin dress, her long hair streaming over her shoulders. Her face was uplifted and her eyes were shining. His astonishment was greatly increased when he saw that she was seated on a plough, in the middle of a ploughed field he knew to be the property of Old Madam. He bade her good-night and she bowed to him and raised her hand on which he saw a diamond ring flashing in the moonlight. When he arrived home he told his relatives he had seen Old Madam, but what on earth was she doing sitting on a plough in the moonlight? He was even more shocked when they told him she had died seven days ago.

Sabine Baring-Gould, who was descended from Old Madam, relates another daylight appearance of her in his *Early Reminiscences* (perhaps the best of his 150 books), as it was told to him by a woman who, as a girl, had seen the ghost of Old Madam in one of her orchards. All the trees were laden with apples and some of the ripest had fallen to the grass, it thus being easy for her to fill her pockets. When these were bulging with stolen apples she suddenly looked up and saw Old Madam watching her and pointing an accusing finger at her. Terrified, she ran as fast as she could to a gap in the hedge, nearly all the apples dropping from her pockets as she did so. She was about to climb through the gap when she saw the ghost of Old Madam for the second time, now standing in front of her, pointing at her pockets until the last stolen apple had been thrown down, when she vanished.

Old Madam's ghost was seen in various parts of the county, always in white, walking over Galford Down, or by the old church, or pausing by the Dew Pond before passing on. As a rule she was not a frightening ghost but was kindly and gentle and became as familiar a sight as if she had been a real live acquaintance. Then a very frightening appearance was made by her. It was in 1832, 37 years after her death, when a young carpenter working in Lew Trenchard church, for some reason (perhaps out of curiosity since he had heard so much of Old Madam) decided to look inside the vault where Old Madam had been buried beside her husband. Suddenly she rose up out of her coffin and chased the unfortunate man all the way back to his home. A bright light streamed from her and threw the man's shadow before him all the way, until she vanished.

Thirty two years later she was seen by a man returning home from Tavistock by night. He saw a white-clad figure which he knew to be Old Madam, seated by a mine-shaft. She might well have been trying to save him from an accident but he was so terrified that he tried to jump aside into a hedge and broke his leg. The story was related by Baring-Gould; he had been invited to dinner by the Rector of Bratton who had told his cook that the Baring-Goulds were to be guests, whereupon the cook, who was the wife of the man who had broken his leg, categorically refused to cook the meal. It was only with the greatest difficulty she was finally persuaded to do so.

In her own house, the beautiful Manor House in Lew Trenchard, which is now an hotel, Old Madam made frequent appearances. She had every right to do so, since she had fought like a tiger during her lifetime to restore prosperity to the estate almost bankrupted by her son. In the Long Gallery the sound of her high-heeled shoes has often been heard, and Baring-Gould tells us that her footsteps were often heard by his mother when the Long Gallery was empty and closed. He himself had given a coming-out ball for one of his daughters and was not at all surprised when many of the guests asked him who was the dark lady in a lace dress moving about freely between the dancers. In fact his own theory was that Old Madam was a spectral transference of another ancestress, Susanna Gould, who had married against her father's wishes and on returning from the wedding ceremony in the church had dropped dead in her white bridal dress. Certainly there was no real reason for Old Madam to be invariably dressed all in white, though the theory is otherwise difficult to understand.

Nevertheless, Baring-Gould knew of various appearances of Old Madam in the Manor House. A certain Mr Twigge staying in the house came down dressed for dinner, and since he was the only guest, was astonished to see two guests sitting in the drawing room. One was seated in an armchair with his back towards him, so that he could only see that he was a gentleman with a wig or powdered hair. Opposite him sat an elderly lady in a white satin dress. Not wishing to disturb them he went on to the dining-room, where his host awaited him. He asked him who the other two guests were. Baring-Gould at once went to the drawing room but it was empty. He then remembered he had been told long before that it had been the custom for Old Madam and Parson Elford of Lew Trenchard to spend Saturday and Sunday evenings together, seated on either side of the fireplace to discuss the services. This was because they and the clerk were the only three able to read. It was the duty of the clerk, when a psalm was given out, to say: 'Let Madam Gould, the Parson and I sing to the praise and glory of God.' What is even more interesting about the apparition is that there was not only the ghost of Old Madam but also the ghost of Mr Elford present, which is quite extraordinary.

The last two visitations of Old Madam in her own house were quite remarkable. When one of Baring-Gould's children was ill the nurse was suddenly awakened one night by a woman's voice sharply saying: 'It is time for her to have her medicine'. She jumped up in panic and opened the door. There was no one there, nor had anyone told her the stories of Old Madam for fear that she might leave if she knew the house to be haunted.

It was as recently as 1918, when one of Baring-Gould's grandchildren was staying with him in the Manor House that Old Madam made her last recorded visitation. There were two nurses in charge of them but both soon gave notice as they had seen an unknown woman bending over the children's beds. It is quite possible that the other servants had told them the house was haunted; they had become quite accustomed to the fact, as it was such a kindly ghost. The nannies were replaced by a Swiss nurse who during her stay neither saw nor heard of any ghost known as Old Madam – perhaps her spectre is now at rest.

THE DREADED GHOST HOUSE

The Ghost House in the Devonshire village of Sampford Peverell provides a classic example of that most cruel, relentless and frightening of all apparitions, known as a *poltergeist*. The German word means a noisy spirit, as indeed it often is. It was in April 1810 that a Mr John Chave decided to take up residence as a tenant in the already renowned haunted house, which had been without a tenant for many years. It belonged to a Mr Talley who was overjoyed to have found a tenant at last and probably let the place at a peppercorn rent to ensure occupation. In those days the exterior of the house was as attractive as all the other cob-built whitewashed cottages in the pretty village near Tiverton, and that was probably the reason for John Chave's choice. He had with him six female servants and all their luggage, so the house would be fully occupied.

Gossip and rumours at once began among those who remembered the old days, when the villagers disliked going near the house in the daytime and avoided it completely at night. They were more concerned for the female servants than for their master. These servants were Mary Dennis senior and junior, Martha Woodberry, Ann Miles, Mrs Pitts and Sally Case. No sooner had everyone settled in on the very first night than all hell broke loose, as the ghost or ghosts gave warning of what was to come. If John Chave had any doubts at all about the house being haunted, he must have been very perturbed at what was happening because he soon became aware of some unusual body or bodies moving noisily about the house.

There were banging doors and the stamping of heavily booted feet moving from room to room and up and down the stairs. The servants gathered together in fear and trembling at the noise for it was quite impossible to sleep. The poltergeists, which judging by their activities they certainly were, were faithfully recorded by the Reverend Caleb Colton in his *Narrative of the Sampford Ghost*, later published during the tenancy of John Chave. The activities were typical of this type of evil spirit or spirits, which have produced numerous hauntings not only in the British Isles but in Europe, America and Canada, being always renowned for their violence, especially towards women and even more towards children.

The poltergeists, having prepared the ground for their new victims, now began to get vicious by beating the maids as they lay attempting to sleep in the one room allotted to them. Mr Chave, who had not himself been attacked or disturbed, decided to call in the local priest, the Reverend Caleb Colton, to try and drive out the spirits by exorcism. If the reverend gentleman failed in his appointed mission, which he assuredly did, he produced the aforementioned astonishing document, recording every single detail that took place in the house from the very first moment he set foot in it.

Ann Miles was the first victim to be picked out by the ghost in a most vicious attack upon her sleeping body with severe beatings as she lay terrified and speechless with fear. Her treatment was the first entry Colton made in his notes as a personal witness of the severe cruelty carried out by the ghost leaving 'a bruise on her face as large as a turkey's egg' as he described it. He had been called in by the terrified screams of the other servants. In order to placate any unpleasant rumours by village gossips he obtained from Ann Miles herself her own statement on oath.

The following night the poltergeist switched his attack to the other defenceless women servants; Mr Chave neither heard their screams nor the noise of the beatings. They were beaten black and blue and were left struggling and screaming for pity and for help. Colton recorded 'that he had heard upwards of two hundred blows upon a bed delivered in one night, the sounds were like that of a strong man striking with clenched fists.' It seems quite incredible for a man to have recorded such details while making no personal attempt to enter the room and try and prevent it, and this throws grave doubts upon the truth of all his subsequent *Narrative*. What is more surprising still is that he did not even call John Chave to do something about it, supposedly fast asleep as he always was. He later wrote of one appalling night of such violence that shrieks of pain came the servants room, with heavy banging from all over the house. The whole incident was faithfully recorded by the priest, who made no notes as to why candles were not lighted in the rooms, and gave no explanation as to why Chave did nothing to stop the brutality. By now all the servants had bruises on their bodies and had made up their minds that they would never sleep in that room again. In fact the more one reads the record left to posterity the more it seems that he was himself watching the flagellation and heard the screams but was powerless to do anything to help.

On that shocking night Chave was forced to summon a surgeon to examine the victims and treat their wounds. Colton called in another man, Mr Sully, an excise officer, to witness statements on oath by all the servants of the treatment they had received. It was only then that Chave said he had heard a lot of noise and had got out of bed to call the Reverend Colton when something snatched the lighted candle and the candlestick out of his hand and flung it across the room.

Chave had now been joined by his wife, who seemed as oblivious of the noise, screams and beatings as her husband. However when they had all settled down for the night the ghosts seem to have turned on both her husband and herself. They were wakened in the night by the heavy curtains of their bed moving violently and jerking on their rings as if being tugged to and fro. When they were forced to get up and investigate they tried to knot them together, but some unseen hand untied the knots and the curtains whirled about as if in a high wind. Mr Chave pressed the bell for a servant, but no one answered. A constant sound of tearing prevented them from sleeping.

New sounds then came into the house, something indefinable like a man's slippered foot coming down the stairs and passing right through the wall. Colton continues the account:

> I have been in the act of opening a door when a violent rapping was heard on the other side of the same door, yet I could swear that no one was there. And again I was in one of the rooms that has a large modern window when from the noises, knockings, blows on the bed, and rattlings of the curtains I really began to think the whole chamber was falling in. Mr Taylor was sitting in the chair the whole time.

Still the Chaves made no move to vacate the house, but a very thorough investigation of every room was made and nothing untoward discovered. Chave actually called in Mr Searle, the governor of the county gaol, to sit up at night with another independent witness and make their own personal investigations of any intruder. Colton recalled another incident in his mystifying document, when he records that a sword was placed upon the bed with a heavy Bible laid on it. It had no sooner been done than both Bible and sword leapt into the air and dashed themselves against the further wall. Mr Taylor, a friend of Colton, hearing a great disturbance and noise, rushed into the room, only to see the sword suspended in the air, its blade pointing towards him before it dropped to the floor.

By now news of what was going on had circulated round the village, and all knew that the poltergeist was once more at work. Their anger was directed against John Chave for allowing his servants to be treated in such a way. Even Mr Talley, the owner of the house, was angry with the Chaves for causing such things to happen, which would make the house impossible to rent to anyone again. Other people believed that Talley was the guilty party and was trying to get rid of Chave for some unknown reason. The *Taunton Courier* published vitriolic attacks in their leaders against the Reverend Colton, who denied all charges vigorously in his own pamphlets. Finally the editor openly accused the Reverend Colton of fraud and of bamboozling and hoodwinking the public. Colton, in yet another pamphlet, denied all charges, emphasising that the noises and disturbances went on to such an extent that all those in the house had finally made up their minds to leave, having been driven out by the ghost or ghosts, and their evil, brutal cruelty towards innocent people.

The strangest mystery of the whole account is how and why these people were able to continue living there for three long years. Most normal people would have been driven insane by such intense noise and cruelty. Even more inexplicable is that it was principally the servants who suffered, being unable to leave because in those days they had to have 'a character' from their former employer to be able to start again in another house and family.

It was over two years before the Reverend Caleb Colton silenced every one, accused and accusers alike, when he published the following statement:

> I may now inform the public, what the newspapers would not, or could not; namely that a reward of £250 has been offered for anyone who can give such information as may lead to a discovery. Nearly two years has elapsed and no claimant has appeared. I myself, who have been abused as the dupe at one time and the promotor of the affair at another, was the first to come forward with £100, and the late mayor of Tiverton has now an instrument in his hands empowering him to call on me for the payment of that sum to anyone who can explain the cause of the phenomenon.

No one ever has claimed the reward. Strangely enough another tenant did rent The Ghost House, a grocer and general dealer who far from ever seeing or hearing anything, flatly refused to believe there ever had been any ghosts.

There is, however, a totally different interpretation of the whole series of events, for during the great days of smuggling The Ghost House was one of a depot used by smugglers, as described by Charles Harper in his splendid book *Haunted Houses*. He himself wrote about it after receiving a letter from The Reverend Philip Rossiter:

> Mrs Chave was alive when we came here... in 1874 but she could not explain anything: only relate what took place. My own idea is, the noises were caused by smugglers; for when I was at Beer in 1876 – taking the duty – I used to visit a very old smuggler – a delightful old man – and he told me many tales of the days of smuggling: how they used to land the spirits on very dark nights, and if pursued by the Revenue Officers take them inland, on packhorses. I asked how far they took their load, and he – not in the least knowing where I came from – said, 'Sometimes we took them as far as Sampford Peverell, and hid some of them in the old tree in the churchyard...'

Berry Pomeroy

If they had taken some of their spirits to the Old Ghost House, they would have wished to frighten people to account for their noise in storing the goods; and sailors in those days were up to all sorts of mischief. It appears at the time that there was a rector here whose brother was Rector of Seaton (adjoining Beer) and they may have helped the smugglers, as it is a well-known fact that many gentry and parsons in those days did so.

In his book *Smuggling 1700 to 1850,* A.D. Hippisley-Coxe adds to Charles Harper's account: 'This indeed is true; the vicars of East Budleigh were intimately connected with smuggling for over a hundred years, and in the thickness of the rectory walls there were two secret passages eighteen inches wide.' This still does not explain the cruelty of the beatings and the episode of the leaping sword and Bible. But then the mysteries of the best ghost stories have never been solved.

THE VIOLENT CASTLE GHOST

Of all the many haunted castles and their ghosts, none is more impressive than Berry Pomeroy Castle near Totnes in Devon. It is a secret place surrounded by dense woods and a moat, and was built in stone by the powerful Pomeroy family in the early 14th century, to replace an earlier wooden castle. Its grim ruins are all splendid remains of fine medieval architecture, especially St Margaret's Tower, the ramparts, drawbridge and portcullis. Standing within its courtyard one can only be astonished that for over six centuries only two great families have possessed it, the Pomeroys and the Seymours. It is privately owned today by the Duke of Somerset, who with the aid of English Heritage has done much to restore it. Today, however, even to stand in that courtyard is to feel a sense of uneasiness when one remembers its grim and terrifying history.

Legend has it that God's wrath descended on the castle for its evil past, and caused it to be destroyed by a fire. The ghosts of two blindfolded horses mounted by armed riders have been seen leaping over the ramparts into the moat below. Two women have also appeared, presaging death within the year to those who see them. Both having died violent deaths themselves are also notorious ghosts. The powerful and ruthless Pomeroy Barons had backed Prince John, later King John, in the wars of the late 12th century against Richard I, the Lionheart. When they learned that the latter, returning from his Crusade, had reached St Michael's Mount on his way to London, the Pomeroy Barons had ordered their horses to be blindfolded, dressed themselves in full armour and ridden to their deaths.

Later in that century another Pomeroy, leaving his castle for wars abroad, had left his younger daughter Margaret in the charge of her sister Eleanor. Eleanor became intensely jealous of her very beautiful sister when they both fell in love with the same man, and she began to plot her sister's murder. She managed to lure Margaret into one of the towers to see what the underground dungeons were like, as they had always been prohibited from going there during their father's residence. She persuaded Margaret to go in first and then suddenly slammed the door on her, and heedless of her desperate cries for help, ran up the stairs to safety, leaving her to starve to death. The tower is named Lady Margaret's Tower after her.

From the moment of her death the tower was haunted by her ghost with its long flowing robes and golden hair, restlessly moving along the castle walls or standing beckoning in a desperate plea for help to those who have seen her. Children will never play near the tower when visiting the castle, though they will play anywhere else. Eleanor's ghost, the manifestation of all that is evil, also haunts, its authenticity confirmed by a most distinguished physician named Dr Walter Farquhar who became deeply involved in both hauntings and recorded all his experiences in his *Memoirs* which he later published.

As a very young doctor he became noted for his skill, to such an extent that he was appointed Physician-in-Ordinary to the Prince Regent, later George IV. All his patients had great trust in him, not only medically but personally, because of his truth and sincerity. He had come to take a short and restful holiday in Torquay when he received an urgent summons to Berry Pomeroy Castle, which he had never visited. It was there that he had his first terrifying encounter with the evil ghost, an experience that he carefully wrote down, becoming so immersed in the supernatural that he wished others to share in his experiences.

It was at the end of the 19th century that these events took place. At that time there were still a few rooms left that could be inhabited amidst the ruins, although the fact that anyone could live there at all with any degree of comfort was certainly strange. What follows is a fully documented account of what happened to him.

On his arrival the doctor was immediately shown into a room and asked to wait while the Steward went to inform his wife that the doctor had come to see her. It was a poorly furnished apartment but with richly panelled walls of dark oak. The only light in the room filtered through the panes of an armorial window blazing with the coats of arms of the Seymour family, which had remained untouched by the fire. There was a great fireplace and dark open steps formed part of a staircase leading to an upper room. These steps were touched by the last gleams of a summer's twilight.

As the minutes passed in the cold room the doctor began to feel annoyed at being left alone for so long. He was by nature a patient man, but as an eminent physician he was not accustomed to being kept waiting, especially after receiving an urgent summons. Just at the moment when he had made up his mind to depart a young woman entered the apartment. The doctor rose to meet her, thinking it was someone come to summon him. To his astonishment she glided across the room quickly, wringing her hands in great anguish, not even glancing at him as she passed. She paused a moment at the foot of the stairs before beginning to climb them in haste and agitation. The doctor, not attempting to follow her, saw her reach the top stair where she paused again and half turned her head towards him, then vanished. In the dim light falling across her face he saw that she was young and beautiful but the eyes of a skilled doctor saw vice and cruelty in her eyes. As he wrote:

> If ever human face exhibited agony and remorse, if ever eye, that index of the soul, portrayed anguish uncheered by hope and suffering without interval, if ever features betrayed that within the wearer's bosom there dwelt a hell, those features and that being were then present to me.

The doctor was stunned by what he had seen and had not heard the Steward, who at the very moment of her disappearance had silently entered, and without apology for his long absence, said his wife was now ready to see him.

He found his patient very ill indeed, so ill that he needed all his knowledge and skill to save her life. He gave her what medicine he had and said that he would return as early as was possible the next morning. On arrival next day he found his patient very much better, and he reassured the Steward that his wife would recover. The strange lady that he had seen the previous day then returned to his mind, and he questioned the Steward as to her identity.

He saw at once the shock and fear in the eyes of the Steward as he mumbled the words 'my wife, my poor wife.' 'Why does this affect her?' asked the puzzled doctor. 'Much. Much.' replied the Steward. 'That it should have come to this… I cannot lose her. You know not the strange and sad history, and his lordship is very adverse to any allusion ever being made to the circumstances, or any importance attached to it. But I must, and will out with it. The figure which you saw is supposed to represent the daughter of one of the Pomeroy Barons who lived in the chamber above. His daughter bore a son out of incestuous intercourse. Filled with horror and shame at what had happened she strangled the child.

'Her appearance', he continued, 'always presaged the death of an inmate of this house. She is always seen dressed in the garments she wore at the time of the crime, with the frenzied gestures and wild look in her eyes that you saw yourself. She even appeared to my wife before my son was drowned some time ago. My poor wife,' he burst out. 'My poor wife. I know she will die. I am sure she will die.' The doctor tried to calm him, 'But I assure you she is not all that ill. I shall come tomorrow as I promised both of you.' The Steward stared at him wildly. 'I have lived in this castle for over thirty years and never known the omen fail.' 'Arguments based on omens are absurd,' replied the doctor as he prepared to leave the room, 'a few days and she will be quite well again. You will see.' They parted equally dissatisfied. He returned to Torquay, but before long a messenger came to say that his patient at the castle had died.

It was this ghost that first interested the doctor in the supernatural and he began a lifelong study of the subject. Many years intervened before he was to hear of a further grim appearance of the Steward's dreaded omen.

The doctor had become even more distinguished in his profession and had been created a Baronet. One day he was visited by a lady who was very concerned about her sister, with whom she and her brother had visited Berry Pomeroy Castle when on a holiday in Torquay. The story she related to him he meticulously recorded in his published *Memoirs* in the following words:

> I am aware of the apparent absurdity of the details which I am about to give to you, but the case will be unintelligible to you Sir Walter without them. While staying at Torquay last summer, we drove over one morning to visit the splendid ruins of Berry Pomeroy Castle. The steward was very ill at the time (he died in fact while we were going over the ruins) and there was some difficulty in getting the keys. While my brother and I went in search of them my sister was left alone for a few moments in a large room on the ground floor and while there, most absurd fancy! she has persuaded herself she saw a female enter and pass her in a state of indescribable distress. The spectre, I suppose I must call her, horribly alarmed her. Its features and gestures have made an impression on her, she says, that no time can efface. I am well aware of what you will say, that nothing can be more preposterous. We have tried to rally it out of her, but the more we laugh at her folly the more agitated and excited does she become. In fact I fear we have aggravated her disorder, by the scorn with which we have treated it. For my own part, I am satisfied her impressions are erroneous, and arise entirely from a deprived state of the bodily organs. We wish for your opinion and are most anxious you should visit her without delay.

The doctor said he would certainly visit her at once, but that she was suffering from no delusion, indeed the spectre was real, and that before he saw her sister he thought it was only proper and helpful to say that he himself had also seen the apparition and that there was no question whatsoever of her either being seriously ill or fabricating the story of what she had seen. He said it was a fact and not a thing to laugh about or disbelieve. Of course she was shocked, as he himself had been, but she would recover under his personal care, and according to his book she did.

THE BEAST OF THE MOORS

Spectral black dogs are numerous in the folklore of England, particularly the savage black hound whose baying strikes terror into the hearts of those who hear him, and who is supposed to bring a warning of imminent death. Howls and bayings are still heard at night on Exmoor, where for years a mysterious and greatly feared animal known as the Beast has roamed, never having been identified. Dead sheep are found as its victims, their throats savagely torn, their bodies covered with blood. It is now over twenty years since tracks of this mysterious animal were first discovered by a farmer near South Molton, with no other signs of an animal.

It was not until one September evening in 1983 that the animal was first seen in this district. Suddenly a farmer saw ahead of him what looked like a huge jet-black cat. It had a round, full face and hard staring eyes, and suddenly vanished. The farmer was convinced this must be the Beast. Other people began to say they had seen a strange animal, but the colours varied from grey-blue, grey, black, jet-black and russet, to the colour of a Labrador. Rumours were now widespread but still none of the sightings had been verified, and it began to become a legend. The shocking reports became real and frightening when one farmer in the area reported that he had lost eighty sheep in about three months, all of them with their throats ripped out, but he never saw the culprit.

The news spread like wildfire, local papers featured it, journalists came down from London; so serious was the threat considered that the Royal Marines were called out to deal with the Beast. Two-man teams of marksmen kept watch night after night to shoot the murderer, but the Beast was neither seen nor killed. By now rumours varied about the animal: it was a panther, a lynx, a puma, even a wolf, each time a different shape or a different colour, large, medium or small, and still the mystery remained.

Other questions began to be asked. Was it a single animal, had it a mate, were there offspring? One of the papers then suggested that

Dartmoor

it might have escaped from a zoo or a private menagerie. This was confirmed by a wild report that a certain butcher in Barnstaple, who had a small private menagerie, had released two pumas, one brown, one nearly black, having been ordered by the police to dispose of them before he left for America. This had been in 1976, seven years before the first recorded sighting of the animal by the farmer in South Molton. Few people, however, could have described the animal they had seen as a puma, unless they had seen one in a zoo or a circus. Some ridiculed the rumours, but for those who had had a sheep killed and its throat torn out the matter was serious; the animal had to be caught or shot. Clairvoyants were unable to discover anything and no witches were known to exist on Exmoor at that time who could have cast a spell. But the terror remained, especially at night when screams were heard from some animal that could only have been the Beast.

Many inhabitants of Exmoor must have been reminded of the famous Sherlock Holmes story of *The Hound of the Baskervilles*, and the hound that haunted nearby Dartmoor. 'A hound it was, an enormous coal-black hound but not a hound mortal eyes have ever seen. Fire burned from its open mouth. Its eyes glowed with a smouldering glare. Its muzzle and hackles and dewlap were outlined in flickering flame.'

To farmers the Beast is a menace, a threat to their livelihood, to be destroyed by whoever sees it. There was, however, a biologist living in Bishop's Nympton, almost at the centre of the area where the killing had taken place, who for some twenty years had quietly but exhaustively studied the antics of the Beast. He has worked with farmers, veterinary surgeons, police and those who think they have seen it, and he has become utterly convinced there is such a Beast, but still there is no concrete evidence of the animal. It requires the most expensive and advanced methods and instruments to sight it, especially by night, and kill it by scientific means.

It is some time now since the last sheep was found dead by a farmer, with its throat torn out. In spite of the long silence people still claim to have heard screams on Exmoor at night and the Beast has now become part of Exmoor legends. But could the Beast have gone to Cornwall? There has been great distress among the farmers around Bodmin Moor, who have had sheep killed by a mysterious animal. Some say it was a huge black cat, and it has actually been photographed (albeit at a distance). Whatever it is, it has caused panic among the agricultural community, enough for them to request that an investigation be carried out by the Ministry of Agriculture. A thorough trace of all paths and tracks and examinations of the sheep that had been killed have been duly carried out, costing thousands of pounds. These investigations revealed no evidence whatsoever that the Beast was even a cat, in spite of photos and videos. In spite of all this, the Cornish farmers still believe there is 'something'.

As one who has treated this beast to be a ghost or spirit, since it has never been seen with accuracy, I was suddenly alerted to an item in *The Independent* newspaper of 2 September 1995, under the heading *A little local trouble – a weekly round-up of rural rumpuses*:

> A new beast was reported this week, but this time on Exmoor. It was spotted chasing sheep on a South Molton farm in the early morning; observers believe it to be a wolverine. These are smallish mammals but famed for their ferocity. In their native US they are said to be able to bring down a galloping moose. The animal was last seen heading towards Combesland. West Country naturalist Trevor Beer said: 'the report seems quite authentic.'

It is not the first time wolverines have been spotted in the West Country; the Welsh National Farmers' Union has put out warnings in the past asking farmers to be on the lookout for the animals.

On 18 November 1995 a sighting of the beast was again reported in *The Independent,* now in Wales, as feared by the Welsh National Farmers' Union:

> An unusually large fox has been killed in Dyfed after being linked to 15 sheep deaths in two weeks. Farmers at Tregaron feared the animal massacring their sheep might have been a big cat, but this was disproved when it was shot. One of them, Ednyfed Jones, said: 'The record for the heaviest fox in Britain is 27lbs. This one was 21lbs, and farmers in the area have never seen a fox so big.'

Since the fox's death, there have been no further reports of sheep killings. The South Molton and Bodmin Moor farmers must be living in hope that no more of their sheep will be lost. But what of the legend? No doubt it will live on forever.

Athelhampton Hall

DORSET

A UNIQUE GHOST

One of the most remarkable ghost stories is that of the mysterious re-appearance, shortly after his death, of a boy complete with his own coffin, to prove that his had not been a natural death as a doctor had evidenced. The story first appeared in detail in the *Gentleman's Magazine* of 1774, and reads convincingly, as if the writer had made a thorough investigation of a case that had happened nearly 50 years earlier.

In May 1728 John Daniel, a fourteen-year-old pupil of Beaminster School who had suffered all his short life from fits, left school because of what was called 'ill of the stone'. A few days later he was missing and a search was made to find him. It resulted in the discovery of his body in a field about a furlong from his distressed mother's home. It seems to have been generally accepted that one of his sudden fits had caused his tragic death and the doctor, in agreement, signed his death certificate. His funeral and burial were duly carried out and apart from the shared sorrow of his death the tragedy was forgotten.

It was about a month later, on Saturday 22 June, that an appalling series of events disturbed the whole village, arousing suspicion and horror around the whole question of John Daniel's death. The schoolmaster had held the usual classes in the gallery of the church, in those days the village school, and at noon he had dismissed his class. All the boys immediately rushed out into the churchyard to play; one of them, who held the classroom key, went back to search for some old pens. On the way, however, he was suddenly frightened by the sound of someone or something booming on a brass pan. He at once rushed back to tell some of the boys and three others joined him to return to the classroom, where all were scared by not only the booming noise but also the sound of a man in very heavy boots. They all ran round the churchyard to the west door where they distinctly heard the voice of the schoolmaster as if he were preaching to a congregation.

By then the news had spread to the other boys who had stopped playing and were moving back to the classroom, but hearing the sounds from the church, all ran away except the boy with the key, who made up his mind to enter the room. As he went into the empty classroom he froze with fear, unable to understand what he saw there. On one of the benches lay a coffin, some six feet in length. Thoroughly alarmed now he rushed back to the other boys to tell them what he had seen and all twelve of them decided to go back to see if what the boy had told them was true. Not only was it true but – even more horrifying – seated on the coffin was a ghostly figure. The silence was broken by a cry from one of the boys: 'There sits our John Daniel with just such a coat on as I have. Look, with a pen in his hand with a book before him. I'm going to throw a stone at him, he's my half-brother.' The other boys, alarmed at what he had said, tried to stop him, but he suddenly cried out: 'Take it!' upon which the ghost and coffin instantly vanished.

It is rare enough to see a ghost in broad daylight, but for all those boys to have seen a ghost of a boy they had known, seated on a coffin as if he were actually in the room, must surely have been one of the most astonishing of occurrences. Even more incredible is that the ghost of the coffin should also have appeared.

Only one of that group of boys had never seen John Daniel because he had not attended the school at the same time, yet this boy was able to add a further detail to the strange story, for he stated that John Daniel's hand had a white bandage on it. Rumours were rife in the village and it became necessary for the coroner, Colonel Broadrep, to make a full investigation. Every boy of the group of witnesses who had seen the ghosts of John Daniel and his coffin was thoroughly questioned and cross-examined as if they had been in a witness box, but there was no doubt whatsoever of the truth of the boys' statements and an exhumation was ordered to be made for verification of all details. Only one woman added a most important detail supporting the boy's story of the white bandage. She had been called in to lay out John Daniel's body and had removed from his hand a white bandage.

Further damning evidence came from the joiner and carpenter who had made the coffin and had seen 'a black list' round the neck of the corpse. A chirurgeon, who was also present, when asked by the coroner for his statement declined to give positive evidence of dislocation of the neck. The verdict of the coroner was not the expected one 'died of natural causes', but the single terrible word, 'strangled'. The verdict came as a great shock to the whole village and no-one was satisfied for there was no proof of, nor reason for the boy's murder. But not one of that group was ever going to forget the sight of the ghost of their playfellow seated on his own coffin, as if he had returned to them in an appeal to see some justice done for his murder. As a ghost story in itself it is decidedly a unique case. His body lies in peace somewhere in the churchyard of that beautiful Beaminster village where once a warning notice read: 'Drive slowly or break your neck'.

THE GHOST SEXTET

Dorset has a great number of ghosts recorded in the county, but probably nowhere more than Athelhampton Hall near Puddletown, not far from Dorchester, where several ghosts have been operating for some centuries. This magnificent Elizabethan mansion, owned by the Martyn family in continuous succession from 1350 to 1595, is supposed to have been built on the ancient site of the palace of King Athelstan. He was the grandson of Alfred the Great and reigned from 924 to 939. The Hall was dearly loved by Thomas Hardy whose father, a builder, did much in the restoration of the building carried out in the 1890s. Thomas Hardy wrote of 'Athelhall' – as he called Athelhampton Hall – in both poetry and prose, and particularly of one of its ghosts, the Grey Lady, whom he called 'the Dame of Athelhall' and who wandered about the Hall and grounds.

Long before that, however, it was the Martyn Ape ghost that haunted the Hall after a great tragedy struck one family. The family arms seem to be everywhere and its crest is

Martyn's Ape

strange enough. It shows an ape seated on a tree stump, holding in its right paw a mirror. The motto is a warning: 'He who looks at Martyn's ape, Martyn's ape shall look at him.'

In the nearby St Mary's church at Puddletown the ape can be seen at the feet of a fine alabaster effigy of Sir William Martyn M.P., Lord Mayor of London in 1503. It is chained to its 'clog', a block of wood intended to impede motion. Also in the Athelhampton Chantry are other members of the Martyn family represented in alabaster, marble, and brass in a very remarkable and impressive chapel. In the south-east corner in another alabaster altar-tomb lie effigies of a knight and his lady, both damaged. They appear to date from the 15th century and the ape at the foot of the knight would certainly mark him as a Martyn. This was at one time a free-standing tomb and is now backed by panelling showing angels holding shields. Another smaller altar-tomb shows a knight in plate armour – presumably a Martyn – and is probably earlier than 1400.

Martyn's Ape – the crest of the family arms at Athelhampton Hall

But it is the statue of Nicholas Martyn, who died in 1595, last of the male line, that is quite superb. He is shown kneeling before an altar. Behind him are his three sons and on his right is his wife Margaret, née Wadham, whose brother founded Wadham College, Oxford, and her seven daughters. His three sons pre-deceasing him, the Martyn male line ceased. According to the Dorset historian Hutchins an epitaph (now illegible) was inscribed with the words:

Nicholas ye first, and Martyn ye last
Good night Nicholas.

The tombs are worth travelling miles to see.

The nearby Athelhampton Hall was built for Sir William Martyn, Knight Bachelor, between 1471 and 1475. Its impressive Great Hall with its ornate timber roof and tall stained glass windows bear the coats of arms of many other families who at one time lived here. They brilliantly light up the whole hall with reds, blues, greens and golds.

There are other rooms such as the Great Chamber, the Green Parlour, the State Bedroom, the Yellow Room, and the Library, now regrettably used as a billiard room. It is a pity that so many rooms are roped off when the Hall is open, making them difficult to see in comfort.

It is through the secret door by the fireplace in the Great Chamber that the terrifying Martyn Ape tragedy began long, long ago. In the panelling by the fireplace was a secret button which, when pressed, caused a small door to open, revealing a flight of stairs leading up to the Long Gallery, at the end of which was another door leading down to a room, more like a cell. It is this cell and the passage that were haunted for a very long time by an ape, who had belonged to one of the Martyn daughters whose lover had left her suddenly and without reason.

The girl, in her frantic misery and sorrow, and knowing the secret button in the panelling, fled to the secret chamber where she took her own life. In her misery she had not noticed that her pet ape had followed her and unable to return to the Great Chamber it starved to death. It is not recorded how or when the two skeletons were discovered, but the legend remains and is reflected in the Martyn Ape and the motto of the family coat of arms.

The other five ghosts are peaceful and mysterious, notably Thomas Hardy's

The secret door at Athelhampton Hall

Dame, known to the Martyns as the Grey Lady. The last time she was seen was in 1975 in the Tudor Room, by a housemaid. She told the owner of the house who himself saw her later passing the door of his own bedroom. Later still, a guide sitting quietly and all alone in one of the rooms, seeing that all the visitors of the day had gone, called out to a lady to tell her that the house was closing. As the guide went over to make sure she was leaving the Grey Lady suddenly vanished. She was also seen by another maid who described her as wearing a long grey dress and a very curious head-dress, which might well have been of the type worn centuries ago.

Another ghost used to haunt the wine cellar who was said to be the cooper of the barrels. A huge grille divided the wine cellar from the outside and some of the locks were said to have come from Newgate Prison, though this would seem to be highly improbable in such a great house. An even quieter ghost was known as the 'hooded monk' and used to wander about the house in a black cassock and a shovel shaped hat. He was thought to be either the ghost of a retired rector, or a priest who was supposed to have been writing a book about the mansion, though this seems as unlikely as the theory of the Newgate Prison locks. Whoever it was, however, behaved like a permanent guest, wandering in and out of the rooms, along the passages, and in the gardens.

The most astonishing ghosts, however, are the duellists. One day long ago a guest of the family, quietly reading in the Great Chamber, quite unaccountably looked up from his book to see the figures of two young men coming from nowhere. They suddenly drew their swords, took up fighting positions and began a duel. So realistic were they that the guest cried out aloud to tell them to stop. As they took no notice he rang the bell for one of the maids but nobody answered. In sheer terror and unable to move he watched the duellists moving swiftly round and across the room until one of them, obviously wounded, fell to the floor, when both of them vanished. Both his host and hostess refused to believe his story, the host actually saying: 'I can't understand what you are talking about, since you have met all the other guests staying here.' Nevertheless the story has been accepted as a legendary one and passed on.

The Hall also has an unsolved mystery. It is carved on the stone door-frame of the library and reads:

Once I loved no one but one
Then I loved M…   1630

Was the writer a man or a woman? Was it the Grey Lady? Was it the Martyn girl who killed herself and left her pet ape to die of starvation, all unknowingly? Were the duellists fighting for the love of M… and was one of them a Martyn? Such things are the basis of the legends and traditions that are so much a part of great families and splendid mansions like Athelhampton Hall.

Although there have been so many ghosts in its history there is no sense of fear around Athelhampton Hall. The gardens in particular are serene and hauntingly beautiful. The long green alleys within their Ham stone walls, the Octagon Pond, the Great Terrace and the peaceful and silent canal are all unforgettable, and nothing could disturb their peace.

THE GRUESOME GHOST

In the year 1845 workmen rebuilding part of St Mary's church in the Dorset village of Tarrant Gunville suddenly came upon a skeleton. More surprising even than that, the skeleton's legs were tied together by a yellow silk ribbon. There was no tombstone and the only means of identification was the yellow ribbon. A few of the very oldest villagers either remembered, or had been told the story that had become a legend, that of a man known to all the local people as 'Old Doggett'. He was steward to Lord Melcombe of Melcombe Regis, who owned the great and splendid mansion of Eastbury; he had betrayed his master, and in remorse shot himself. What the whole village could not understand was how, in those days, he had been buried in consecrated ground after committing suicide. His gruesome ghost has haunted the neighbourhood ever since, causing much fear by day and by night.

In 1717 Sir John Vanbrugh started building Eastbury, the magnificent mansion with its great park in the village of Tarrant Gunville, commissioned by George Dodington. No expense was spared by this flamboyant and eccentric man. His wanton extravagance was due– it was rumoured – to money he had obtained from the Admiralty by illegal means. Three years later he died, leaving his estate and £30,000 to his nephew George Bubb Dodington. He was even more of an eccentric than his uncle. He was an M.P., created Lord Melcombe of Melcombe Regis, and began to run through the £30,000 as fast as he could. By the time Eastbury was finished, in 1738, it had cost £140,000, a vast fortune in those days and double the price paid to Vanbrugh for building it.

An enormous portico of columns formed the entrance to the house for the many visitors who came to see Lord Melcombe. They were entertained with ostentatious pomp and ceremony, forced to pass through a whole series of rooms, all lavishly furnished. At the very end they might, or might not, have been taken into his bedchamber in the centre of which stood a specially made four-poster bed canopied with peacock feathers. He had a large wardrobe full of the most elegant and expensive suits. In addition to all those ostentatious extravagances he had a splendid villa in London at Hammersmith which he had named *La Trappe*.

The cost of running Eastbury alone increased more and more, to such an extent that it became impossible to continue the maintenance of the property, both inside and outside. He was finally obliged to offer free residence and a salary of £200 a year to a caretaker. There were many applicants but as soon as they had been escorted through the house they refused to undertake such a prodigious task. Eventually the mansion was sold.

Lord Melcombe, however, had a steward named William Doggett whose task was to guard the premises during the long and frequent absences of his master, who quite often did not even announce his departure from Eastbury or his return, so that 'Old Doggett', as he soon became called by the locals, had a completely free hand in running the huge mansion standing within its acres of parkland. He became a local jest because he always wore breeches tied with bright yellow ribbons, and there was a rapidly developing suspicion of his craftiness in all that he did.

He had a brother who, in serious financial difficulties, appealed to him to help him avoid bankruptcy. This help was willingly given since William had already begun illegally to sell parts of the building materials left around the house. These had been ordered by Lord Melcombe at various times to carry out further improvements to the house.

The two brothers operated mainly at night when all the villagers were asleep. They even paid one of the workmen on the side to do the selling for them as a bonus to the nominal wage. 'Old Doggett' reckoned he could repay some of the profit to Lord Melcombe on his return to Eastbury, though he had no knowledge whatsoever of his master's whereabouts, even had there been an emergency requiring his immediate return. What was being done was nevertheless no secret to the local people, so 'Old Doggett's reputation was not at all good, and many of the villagers were wondering what Lord

Melcombe would do when he found out. They were to know sooner than they thought, for he unaccountably returned unannounced to Eastbury.

The sudden arrival of his master driving up to the mansion in his coach and horses brought panic to 'Old Doggett', for there was no time to work out what he owed his master for all his illegal sales, nor to invent an explanation for the dwindling stock of materials. All he did know was that his debt was by now very considerable. Without a word of welcome to his master he went straight to his room and shot himself. It is said that the blood from his body left a stain on the floor that could never be removed. He was buried, strangely enough for suicides in those times, in consecrated ground in the churchyard of Tarrant Gunville. Almost within hours his gruesome hauntings began. On the stroke of midnight, his ghost was seen wandering on the road as if waiting for a coach and still wearing breeches tied with the bright yellow silk ribbons that he always wore.

After Lord Melcombe's death Eastbury was sold to the Duke of Buckingham and later demolished, only one wing remaining to be used as tenements for the workers. All through those years 'Old Doggett's' hauntings never ceased. Sometimes he was seated in a coach with four headless horses. At other times he himself was headless, only his yellow silk ribbons distinguishing him. He would be seen walking distractedly round the park and along the road up to the entrance portico, but most of all in the house, as if searching for the demolished room where he had taken his life. His ghost is an unusual one in the history of ghost stories and legends, but strangest of all is that his exhumed skeleton after more than a century still had its legs bound together by the yellow silk ribbons. No other witness was necessary to identify him as 'Old Doggett'.

THE SCREAMING SKULL

There are two screaming skulls in the West Country, one, perhaps the more famous, in Somerset, the other in Dorset. The second belongs to Bettiscombe Manor House in the beautiful Marshwood Valley between Broadwindsor and Lyme Regis. For some inexplicable reason only the top half of the skull remains. One theory as to its origins begins with the infamous Judge Jeffreys, whose ghost still haunts Lyme Regis, where he sentenced so many to death after the battle of Sedgemoor and the defeat of the Duke of Monmouth by the Royalist army of James II.

The screaming skull of Bettiscombe Manor

During this period Bettiscombe Manor House belonged to a staunch Puritan, the Reverend John Pinney, who held the living of Broadwindsor and was also an accomplished lacemaker. He had two sons, John and Azariah, who in 1685 took part in the Monmouth Rebellion, were captured and taken to Lyme Regis to be sentenced by the brutal Judge Jeffreys. John was executed. Azariah was sold as a slave and transported for life to the island of Nevis in the West Indies, where his skill as a lacemaker that he had inherited from his father was both useful and profitable to his owner, and made life easier for him.

During those years of slavery he gradually grew rich enough not only to buy his freedom but also to have his own slaves. His grandson, a rich man, returned to Dorset to the old family home, Bettiscombe Manor House, bringing with him a negro servant. This must have caused astonishment, even awe to the villagers, who had never seen a black man. His life became very difficult from the moment he arrived. Furthermore the English climate had disastrous effects upon him, and he soon died of consumption. On his deathbed he said his spirit would never rest until his body was returned to his native country, but in spite of his last wish the body was buried in

Broadwindsor churchyard as it would have been well-nigh impossible in those times to send his body back to the West Indies. What is totally inexplicable is why his skull, or the top part of it, was hidden in the manor house, for even in those bloodthirsty times severing the head from the body was unusual.

If the negro servant's last wish was ignored, his statement that his spirit would never rest was almost at once dramatically realised.

The grounds of the manor house were now being farmed, and the labourers were the first to feel the effects of what had become a curse on the house and lands. They began to leave because of the terrifying screams from the house, as well as banging doors and other noises. The angry farmer threw the skull into the pond, but the house could not be lived in for the screams night and day, and he was forced to drain the pond, dig out the skull and bring it back into the house. As farmers and tenants changed over the years the screaming skull passed into legend. If ever it was moved from the house the screams would begin, the crops would fail, the pigs die of swine fever and the cows would dry.

Quite serious investigations were made but failed to find any solution. It was even suggested that the negro's body had never been buried at all, that he had been murdered and his head cut off to prevent detection. What is not to be doubted is that the notoriety of the screaming skull of Bettiscombe Manor House has passed into legend, not only in Dorset but far beyond and even today its activies are still being recorded.

ANOTHER EVIL GHOST

Few of the West Country ghosts are more evil than that of 'Bloody' Judge Jeffreys. The area is haunted not only by his own frightening ghost but by the ghosts of countless prisoners sentenced by him to be hanged, or perhaps worse, to be sold as slaves. The counties of Somerset and Dorset suffered the most. In Taunton Castle the barbaric judge dealt with 526 cases with not a single reprieve, declaring at the close of his assizes 'that the town was fortunate that he had not depopulated it.' He continued his dreaded assizes throughout the two counties, notably in Dorchester and Lyme Regis.

It is in Lyme Regis that his ghost has so often been seen, where he condemned 12 people of the town to be hanged, drawn, and quartered. The night before the trial he had dined well in the Great House which once stood in Broad Street. His ghost still haunts the spot, some say gnawing a bloody bone. Dorchester suffered even more from the evil judge, and the black oak chair in which he sat to deliver his terrible punishments is in the town's museum.

The harsh and barbaric punishments were passed on simple people, men of conscience and loyalty to a cause, who had been implicated in the Monmouth Rebellion of 1685. The Duke of Monmouth's army consisted mainly of such rebels, ill-armed, ill-disciplined, totally inexperienced, pitted against the royal army of James II in a battle which took place on Sedgemoor on 6 July 1685. The Duke of Monmouth, bastard son of Charles II and Lucy Walter, claimed his right to the English throne, landing at Lyme Regis with a handful of supporters, then heading for Taunton where he was proclaimed king by Protestant adherents. James II had only been on the throne four months but his army crushed the rebels at one stroke, forcing them to flee in all directions; many of them were killed or wounded on the battlefield, decidedly more fortunate than those who were captured and led away as prisoners, and lined up before the cruel Royalist Colonel Kirke, who was as barbaric as the 'Bloody Judge' himself. He ordered them to be chained in gangs and force-marched to Taunton Castle, where the assizes would be held on 17 September. At the end of the first day of horrific sentences passed, Colonel Kirke selected twelve to be hanged on the signboard of the White Hart Inn, on the corner of a street near the assize court. Thus he could see the hanging carried out properly as he dined in the inn.

Many are the ghosts of those the Judge sentenced in Somerset and Dorset, particularly the former, and there could be many more souls lying in unquiet graves in those places they were sent to as slaves. On and around Sedgemoor most of the ghosts are seen when heavy mist and fog obliterate everything on the Somerset levels, as it did on the night before the battle and in the following dawn when a pistol shot triggered the confusion of battle. Monmouth commanded Lord Grey to head the cavalry while he led the foot, riding at their head, but in one of the worst battle betrayals in history both leaders fled and left the rebels to their fate. Monmouth was later captured cowering in a ditch, taken to London and executed on Tower Hill.

Today when the dense fogs and mist cover Sedgemoor, the ghost of Monmouth riding furiously on his grey horse has often been seen. As recently as fifty years ago a London journalist, forced to drive slowly in dense fog, suddenly braked to avoid hitting a horseman on a charger. The charger was standing still as if to let him pass, then suddenly overtook him, jumped a bridge and vanished, leaving the journalist terrified when he realised he had seen a ghost, learning later from locals that it was the ghost of Monmouth.

The ghosts of the dead, wounded, or hanged rebels have more often been seen. Six of the rebels, three from each village nearest to Sedgemoor, were hanged in chains from an oak tree called the Hanging Tree, or Heddon Oak, to warn any passers-by of what a rebellion against the king meant. Local people have heard the rattle of chains and the whispering of ghosts as they hurried past, and even horses gallop faster at the sounds. After the tree was felled in 1979 local people still heard the ghosts. One boy was hanged on an elm tree, near a farm in Walton near Stroud. He was the son of the farmer and was hanged before his father's eyes, condemned by the 'Bloody' Judge in spite of the father selling everything he possessed to defend him.

A similar punishment was meted out to Samuel Sweet, not by Judge Jeffreys but by Lord Feversham, on the Judge's orders. Sweet was claimed as the Champion Runner of Sedgemoor and had fought under Monmouth. To prove his claim he was stripped naked and roped to a wild colt. But after a long run he collapsed and was hanged, drawn and quartered in front of the girl he loved. Her ghost was often seen, wringing her hands with grief for her lover, whose brutal death had sent her mad.

A far more sinister ghost was that of the widow of John Plomley, who as an officer in Monmouth's army had survived being killed, but was widely sought by spies. Both his sons had been caught and hanged, and he himself had been hidden for some time in Cheddar caves until the coast was clear for him to return home to Lockley Manor, near Weston-super-Mare. He had not been there long before he must have been seen, or his presence given away to the Royalists, for troopers were sent to search the house. His wife, holding his pet white spaniel in her arms, watched as they beat their way along the panelling until they found a hollow one. His spaniel jumped out of his mistress's arms and began frantically barking, thus betraying his master who was captured and taken to Taunton to confront the merciless judge. His wife was ordered to accompany him. She dressed herself in her finest clothes, wearing the famous Plomley jewels and sitting impassively until the inevitable sentence was passed; to be hanged, drawn, and quartered. The sentence was carried out before her, and only then did she break down. She was sent back to her home where she flung herself down a forty-foot well in the grounds. The well was not discovered for many years and then only because of excavations in converting the manor into flats. Her ghost has been seen many times round the site of the well and in the grounds, as has the ghost of the white spaniel.

Having dealt with Somerset, 'Bloody' Judge Jeffreys set out for Dorset and Dorchester, where his assizes were to be held. A great number of Monmouth's rebel supporters had come from Dorset, and those who had survived the battle of Sedgemoor had returned to their homes in various parts of the county, but were soon discovered by the king's men. There are many individual ghosts of those who were caught in their own town or village, where they were hanged on trees, in their homes or from church towers. Those who were sent to be tried in Dorchester assizes received the ultimate sentence; to be hanged, drawn, and quartered.

The church of St Mary in Beaminster was one of the first to be defiled when a number of local and village rebels for the Monmouth cause were first hanged, then hoisted up the west tower as a warning to all others who chose to defy the King. The tower is one of the most spectacular in the county and the brutalised bodies could be seen from far and wide. Lyme Regis was the next to suffer when 13 men were hanged, drawn, and quartered. Among them were two youths; William Hewling, who was carried to his grave by the highest-born women of the town, and Christopher Battiscombe, regarded as 'Dorset's model gentleman'. His sweetheart threw herself at the feet of the 'Bloody' judge, imploring him to be merciful, but was waved away. All lie buried in the parish churchyard. In the village of Poynington others were condemned to death when the judge held his court in one of the houses next to the church, belonging to a member of the ancient Cheneys family, one of whom was sentenced.

It was in the fine town of Dorchester that Judge Jeffreys revealed his total lack of mercy. The black oak chair in which he sat during his unforgettable assizes court may still be seen in the museum. No less than 300 rebels were brought to trial, of whom 293 received the usual sentence. Of this number 74 were selected to be hanged, drawn, and quartered within the town walls where people were heartless enough to witness brutal executions.

Yet one more recorded supplication was made to the foul judge, by Dame Alice Lisle who lived in Moyles Court, near Ellingham. She had been arrested and brought to the assizes. The whole countryside had been overrun by those rebels who had escaped capture and certain death. Two of these had gone to her house to beg for sanctuary, even for a short time, until they could be more certain of escaping capture. Dame Alice may well have been a Royalist, but she was also a Christian and agreed to shelter them until it was safe to come out of hiding. The victims had been followed, however, and the King's men arrested both them and Dame Alice and took them to the Assize Court.

In spite of the fact that several of the gentry and notables petitioned for Dame Alice to be released, the Judge decided she had betrayed King James and charged her with high treason, a capital offence, and sentenced her to be hanged. For years her ghost haunted Moyles Court. Her shoes were heard clattering along the corridors and in the rooms. People also reported hearing the sound of rustling silk as her dress swept over the floor. Often people spoke of seeing her seated in a driverless coach drawn by headless horses.

In a very short time Judge Jeffreys had annihilated over one thousand men, women, and children by capital punishment of the most barbarous nature, and had sold an unrecorded number into slavery. Is it, therefore, in any way surprising, that the most pitiless judge in the history of England should have haunted Somerset and Dorset for so long?

Berkeley Castle

GLOUCESTERSHIRE

THE HAUNTED MANSION

To see the haunted mansion for the first time is an unforgettable experience: starting through pillared gates and descending down a very uneven track in a secret and beautiful valley, one is suddenly confronted with the forgotten and unfinished stone edifice of Woodchester Park Mansion. It stands isolated in its 28 acres of parkland with five hidden lakes, and casts an immediate spell over the beholder. In the enfolding silence and peace it is not surprising to find that ghosts have been, and still are there, for there is a strange and eerie sense about the mansion.

One of the earliest and most unusual ghost is that of the Roman soldier pacing up and down in front of the gates or wandering about the park and the mansion. Sometimes he has been seen accompanied by a ragged dwarf, probably his slave, as many of the early Britons were enslaved when the Roman legions occupied Britain, especially in Gloucestershire. As a result of these sightings local people have even warned visitors to the area not to go anywhere near the park or mansion. They describe the place as 'spooky', frightening, even dangerous, and are quite serious about it. They offer as proof the state of the uninhabited mansion, devoid of all its windows, with boarded up rooms marked DANGER, and a vandalised and desecrated chapel 'where strange things have gone on.'

Woodchester Park Mansion was built on or near the site of a large Roman camp. In the 4th century the site covered some thousand acres, in the centre of which stood a magnificent sixty-room villa. In the villa's huge courtyard was a wonderful mosaic of a million pieces depicting Orpheus playing on his pipe to the animals and birds, and part of this mosaic is now in the British Museum. Much of the villa was demolished when the Roman legions were recalled to defend Rome. Is the ghost that of a Roman soldier who deserted from his legion because he loved the place and wished to stay? Whatever the truth his presence as a ghost has been reported throughout the centuries and accepted as a genuine ghost by locals, but the hauntings do not end there.

Before his death the distinguished Earl of Ducie had built a Georgian house for himself in 'Spring Park', as it was then known, on or near to the original Roman site. His son inherited the house and was a great womaniser, extravagant, and rich enough to entertain lavishly during the time he lived there. His departure was sudden and dramatic. He had organised a great dinner party one night where the guest of honour was one of his many lady loves. She was already seated in the chair at his right hand at the head of the table. He himself, as always, was the last to enter the room, waiting for the expected applause before moving towards the table and his seat, when to his horror he suddenly saw his recently dead father sitting there. In shock and horror he rushed out of the room and shortly afterwards from the house, which remained abandoned and unoccupied except for the ghost until 1845 when William Leigh bought it. He was the son of a wealthy Lancastrian merchant who had died and left a considerable fortune. On his conversion to Roman Catholicism he had been cold-shouldered to such an extent by all his friends that he set about searching for another part of the country where he could pursue his beliefs and build a suitable religious building. Woodchester Park Mansion was exactly what he was looking for.

He at once employed the celebrated architect Pugin, but soon quarrelled with him over the enormous expense required to convert the mansion into a religious house. He was utterly determined, however, to build a monastery, and all work on the mansion was deferred until 1854 while he concentrated on his monastery nearby. He had already invited the Venerable Dominic Barberi, Superior of the Passionists Order in Rome. The invitation was duly accepted and both the Superior and some of his monks subsequently arrived and were probably housed in the mansion, Leigh himself going to live in The Cottage, on top of the hill overlooking the mansion, while the work continued.

During these years his health had deteriorated and the costs of the building had risen alarmingly. He died in 1873 aged seventy. Reports were soon circulating locally of new ghosts. Two monks were seen wandering about the grounds, even though all of them and the Superior had returned to Italy. One of them was said to have been that of Dominic Barberi himself. Another monk was said to have committed suicide in one of the hidden lakes. Black dogs were also seen, usually regarded as animals who give warnings of death, appearing near the monastery and in the grounds of the mansion. The mansion was never really lived in and all work on it was suspended. In one of the rooms the stonemason's ladder may still be seen. Some of the rooms were capacious but the most beautiful is the glorious vaulted chapel. Otherwise every window has been vandalised and smashed, and the stables are deserted. The imposing bell-tower, stone gargoyles and splendid facade guard the sole inhabitants, a colony of rare horseshoe bats.

There were other sightings after Leigh's death, one of them Leigh himself rushing about the grounds on a horse. Another was of a keeper who had been savaged by guard dogs used by Leigh to protect his mansion. But of all the ghosts the most authentic are those of American soldiers who, during World War Two, had occupied Woodchester Park for 'most secret and important work' to be carried out there. What this was has never been revealed. There was supposed to have been a secret scientific laboratory in one of the rooms but this is not now evident. There is certainly a room containing a quantity of old X-ray material that has never been removed, and there are rumours that the mansion might have been used as a hospital, but looking at it as it is today this is impossible to believe. Nevertheless the 'sighting' of American soldiers has been reported a number of times quite convincingly.

The mansion has been bought by Stroud District Council with the help of English Heritage, and is being managed by the Woodchester Mansion Trust, who have Open Days for visitors. Information may be obtained from Nympsfield Post Office, Gloucestershire.

BERKELEY CASTLE

In a splendid position, Berkeley Castle was originally built during the 12th century as a great fortress and, inhabited by the Berkeley family, is the oldest inhabited castle in England. Since its construction a series of unpleasant and sinister events have taken place in and around its walls, dominated by the brutal murder of Edward II. As long ago as the year before the Norman invasion the chronicler William of Malmesbury gave an account of the notorious Berkeley Witch haunting the countryside.

> There resided at Berkeley a woman addicted to witchcraft and skilled in ancient augury; she was excessively gluttonous and perfectly lascivious, setting no bounds to her debaucheries. She was not old, though fast declining in life. On a certain day, as she was regaling herself, a jack-daw, which was a very great favourite, chattered a little more loudly than usual. On hearing which the woman's knife fell from her hand, her countenance grew pale, and deeply groaning, 'This day,' said she, 'my plough has completed its last furrow; today I shall hear of, and suffer some dreadful calamity.'

The keep, Berkeley Castle

At the moment that she spoke a messenger arrived from the village and told her that her whole family in the village had died from a sudden accident. She at once took to her bed and sent for her remaining son, a monk, and her daughter, a nun. To them she confessed her witchcraft, and that finally the evil spirits had taken over her soul so that the earth would not receive her. She begged, therefore, that they should carry out her last wishes on her death.

They were to sew up her corpse in the skin of a stag and lay it on its back in a stone coffin, which had to be fastened with lead and iron clasps. Upon this they must lay a stone all bound round with three iron chains, 'of enormous weight'. If she lay secure for three nights her body was to be buried on the fourth day. They obeyed her wishes, but all in vain, for the evil spirits that their mother had feared took control in death as in life. According to William of Malmesbury:

...on the first two nights... the devils, one by one, with the utmost ease bursting open the door of the church, though closed with an immense bolt, broke asunder the two outer chains; the middle one being more laboriously wrought, remained entire. On the third night, about cock-crow, the whole monastery seemed to be overthrown from its very foundation, by the clamour of the approaching enemy. One devil, more terrible in appearance than the rest, and of loftier stature, broke the gates to shivers by the violence of his attack. The priests grew motionless with fear, their hair stood on end, and they became speechless. He proceeded, as it appeared, with haughty step towards the coffin, and calling on the woman by name, commanded her to rise. She replying that she could not on account of the chains: 'You shall be loosed,' he said, 'and to your cost' and directly he broke the chain, which had mocked the ferocity of the others, with as little exertion as though it had been made of flax. He also beat down the cover of the coffin with his foot, and taking her by the hand, before them all, he dragged her out of the church. At the doors appeared a black horse, proudly neighing, with iron hooks projecting over his whole back, on which the wretched creature was placed, and immediately, with the whole party, she vanished from the eyes of the beholders; her pitiable cries for assistance, however, were heard for nearly the space of four miles.

The legend of The Witch of Berkeley is traditional, but there is another, perhaps even more frightening legend. It was that of a huge and repulsive toad which was kept in a well in the castle keep. The existence of this fabulous creature was first recorded by John Smith of Nibley, Steward of the Berkeley Hundred in which Berkeley Castle stood. He wrote of it as being 'a foot neere 16 inches and of incredible bigness and had doubtless lived more than divers hundred of years.' It fed upon the carcasses of slaughtered animals and captured prisoners flung down from above, and from it a horrible stench arose into the cell above. It was in this cell that one of history's most brutal murders took place, that of Edward II.

The king had married Isabella of France who had been remarkably loyal towards this weak son of a strong father. As a soldier he was without any distinction and lost the vital battle of Bannockburn to the Scots. It was not until the country had begun to be virtually ruled by his male favourites, known as 'the king's men' that she abandoned her husband to become the paramour of Roger Mortimer, leaving her husband with his homosexual companions, first the Despensers and then Piers Gaveston.

Both the Queen and Mortimer began to take their revenge, imprisoning the king and moving him from castle to castle until he was finally confined in Berkeley Castle, where it was decided to murder him 'for some swift conclusion to the matter' as the Queen expressed it.

On that fatal night of 13 September 1327 Sir Thomas Gurney and Sir John Maltravers entered the stinking dungeon where the king was imprisoned. They forced the king, who was physically a powerful man, downwards between two mattresses, 'then a kind of horn or funnel was thrust into his fundament through which a red-hot spit was run up into his bowels.' His shrieks were heard far beyond the castle walls and across the countryside on that dreadful night. They are even said to be heard on the anniversary of this date even now. His lover the Lord Despenser was castrated, disembowelled, hanged, drawn and quartered. The king's body was refused for burial by both the Abbots of Bristol and of Malmesbury for fear of the queen's terrible temper, but he was finally buried as a martyr in Gloucester Cathedral.

When Edward III came to the throne Lord Berkeley was summoned to Parliament to explain his absence from his castle on the night of the murder. He asserted that he was but five miles away on that night and his statement was accepted by the king. His steward Smyth later stated that from all the evidence available in the household books his master was most certainly present in his castle. The memory of this terrible murder is kept alive down to this day by the thousands of visitors to Berkeley Castle who never fail in their intention of seeing the actual dungeon where the events took place. Incredibly no record exists of any ghost of the king being seen in or outside the castle.

There is another ghost said still to be seen in the castle grounds. During the Wars of the Roses a bitter and long-running quarrel between William, Lord Berkeley, and Viscount L'Isle, his cousin, finally came to a head. The argument was over certain lands which Lord Berkeley claimed in right of his grandmother, Margaret Beauchamp, Countess of Shrewsbury, against Viscount L'Isle's assertion that such lands were his, though no proof was evident. The fierce altercation was supported on both sides by their followers, and finally led to a fixed battle. By that time the feud had gone on between the two families for some forty-five years.

The battle took place at Nibley Green, about two miles west of Dursley and within the Berkeley Hundred. It was in the year 1469, and Viscount L'Isle lost his life, an arrow being shot through his mouth. It was the last battle to be fought between feudal lords in England. Viscount L'Isle's ghost has been seen many times since – even as late as the last century according to one witness – on the actual site of the battle, between Dursley and the Tynedale Monument.

Chilton Cantelo Farmhouse

SOMERSET

THE POSSESSIVE FARMHOUSE SKULL

The similarity between the Dorset skull in Bettiscombe Manor House, also described in this book, and the Somerset one in Chilton Cantelo Farmhouse is quite remarkable. Theophilus Broome died at the age of 69 on 16 August 1670, and was buried in the north transept of St James, Chilton Cantelo, where his tomb may still be seen. The coat of arms on his tomb, black with a silver chevron and three sprigs of broom, marks him as a Royalist supporter of Charles I, though it is recorded that he was so sickened by the atrocities caused by the Royalists that he defected to the Roundheads. He requested that his head be severed from his body after his death, and instructed his sister that whatever happened the skull must be kept in the house.

During the years after his death there were constant changes of tenants in the farmhouse due to the noises made by the skull, for each time it was removed noise broke like a storm on the whole house. Successive tenants were obviously warned about this, and it was widely known even out and beyond Chilton Cantelo. However there came a day when a tenant in residence, unable to bear the noise whenever he tried to move the skull, decided to investigate and find whether Theophilus Broome had in fact been decapitated. To do this would require an exhumation of his body. So persistent was he about this that the sexton of St James church was authorised to start digging up the grave, which naturally concerned him greatly. The tomb however could not be opened without further permission from the church authorities. When this was given the sexton continued with his work but his spade broke in half. So convinced was he this was an omen that he at once refused to go on with the work. He vowed it was a judgment on him for interfering with the dead. So once again the skull was returned to the house and the angry tenant, but peace was restored.

In 1826, however, when alterations and repairs were being carried out in the farmhouse, the workmen, quite without malice, used the skull as a vessel to hold their tea when it was made, or their beer, something that had happened when our ancestors did the same with the skulls of the prisoners they had captured as headhunters. The skull evidently approved of this practise for it certainly made no protest or noise, and it was safely returned to its cabinet where it may be seen to this very day. My wife and I visited Higher Chilton Farm where we were received with much courtesy and allowed to take a photograph of the skull. So far from ever intending to remove it the occupants were deeply grateful to it for personal reasons, and in a very special way.

Before her marriage Mrs Kerton had visited the house one night and was perturbed at the prospect of living in a house containing a skull. When it was time to leave and get into her car her future husband, seeing a black shadow thought she had dropped her coat and called to her. It was not her coat but the top of an uncovered well. Had she not paused at his call she would have fallen into the well and been killed.

THE GHOST TRAIN

The *Taunton Chronicle* of 26 August and 12 September 1857 gave full reports of a most serious railway accident in Somerset on the West Somerset Mineral Railway at Kentsford, when an engine left Roadwater with a truck carrying about thirty labourers returning to Watchet for their pay. On reaching Washford, Henry Giles, the crossing-keeper, held up his flag and stopped the train, warning the driver not to proceed as a coal train was shortly expected from Watchet. John James, the assistant engineer, was riding on the engine.

After close-questioning the crossing-keeper, and because he had urgent letters to post, James decided they should go on. Giles climbed on to the buffer beam, and the train proceeded at 20 mph. They suddenly saw the coal train about 200 yards away and whistled loudly but were unable to avoid a head-on collision. Both engines were seriously damaged and a month passed before another engine could replace them. Giles was killed instantly, James and another dying of their wounds later, and several others were severely injured and badly scalded by escaping steam. The coroner, after a hearing lasting three days, brought in a verdict of manslaughter against James.

These facts might have remained in the railway records, but they became public in Kentsford in a very unusual manner, for in 1901 curious gossip and rumours were emerging about hearing the sound of a train and the voices of children happily laughing together. The rumours became more frequent just before World War I, when one or two people swore they had heard a train rushing along the rails that by now had been torn out to make munitions, but still they were disbelieved, even laughed at.

It was not until then that one local villager swore he had not only heard the sound of a train but had actually seen it one night. He insisted that he was not just imagining things, because he did not even believe in unnatural objects or ghosts. The matter became more serious when local people said they had heard cries, as if people had been wounded somewhere and were being brought to a local hospital. The most convincing story came from a man who was prepared to swear on oath that he had one night seen a train rushing along, its fire burning brightly as the stoker shovelled on coal.

A few years after the war a postman and his friend who were both in the local brass band and had obviously heard all the rumours and gossip about the phantom train, decided to investigate and find out for themselves what it was all about. One night after they had finished their band practice and were going home, they were about to cross over the bridge when they both saw a tank engine drawing trucks soundlessly reaching the bridge and vanishing. In great fear and astonishment, and not wishing to be jeered at, they agreed to tell no one what they had seen, but after a day or two of talking it all over they decided to tell a reporter of the local paper.

From the day the paper head-lined the story, the village and beyond buzzed with gossip and interest. Those who had spoken before about what they had seen and heard, and been laughed at for their stories, now considered their fears confirmed, while those who had kept quiet about their sightings to avoid ridicule, now told their stories to the paper. Shortly after the article had appeared, a man deeply interested in the occult came to see the two men, heard the whole story, was utterly convinced they told the truth and arranged that all three should spend the night watching for the ghost train. The first two nights nothing happened to disturb them. Even the investigator was prepared to give up, but was persuaded by the other two to give it another chance. It was a bitterly cold February night and by three o'clock in the morning they were frozen and totally dispirited, when suddenly one of them gave a great cry as he saw a lighted engine cab ahead of them and the clear shape of a train approaching them at a speed of about 20 mph. As it approached the bridge the investigator craned forward to see the train pass below the bridge and vanish.

There was no longer any doubt that they had seen the ghost train, all three of them, on the same night and at the same time. To prove it they swore an affidavit before a notary, and the news hit front pages all over the country. Reporters arrived from all over, asking for confirmation and looking for more stories. Then like all hot news it died away, for the train was never seen again. Of all the ghostly objects in the history of the occult the ghost train is the rarest. It was an unknown railway enthusiast that personally studied all the railway records to find the original train, eventually validating every detail of the ghost train.

THE ARTHURIAN GHOSTS

During the sixth century, the Arthurian period, the site of Cadbury Castle was occupied by an ancient Briton chieftain who, with stone and timber, reinforced what was then a hill fort and built a powerful stronghold. According to local legend and tradition this became the home of King Arthur, 'the once and future king' of the immortal story, and the castle itself became known as Camelot. Locally the belief still persists that the hill on which the ruins of the castle stand is haunted by King Arthur and his knights, who make their appearance every seven years on Midsummer Eve. In Somerset in particular, the belief in the great Arthurian legend is an undying and integral part of local folk-lore, and even in very recent times people round Cadbury in Somerset have claimed to see the ghosts of King Arthur and his knights emerging from Cadbury Castle.

The castle stands on a yellow limestone hill which is believed to be hollow, overlooking South Cadbury and visible for miles around across the beautiful Somerset countryside. A causeway once ran across the great marshes below the ramparts of the castle, and is marked on maps even today as King Arthur's Hunting Causeway.

In 1966 a serious attempt was made to prove that Cadbury Castle was in fact Camelot, the legendary palace of King Arthur. The first members of the team set out from the spot known as Arthur's Well, not only with enthusiasm but with the absolute conviction that this would prove to be one of the most important archaeological excavations of all time, settling once and for all the arguments over the old legend. On the very first day therefore it was not surprising to one of the students when a very old man indeed came up to him and seriously and solemnly asked 'Have you come to take away our king?'

It is to Arthur's Well, according to a centuries-old legend, that King Arthur brings his horses from Cadbury Castle to water them at certain times of the day or late evening.

Glastonbury Tor

It is, however, on Midsummer Eve that the whole ghostly army of knights has been repeatedly seen through the centuries by the nearby villagers of North and South Barrow, issuing from the hollow hill on which the castle stands, led by King Arthur himself, their lance heads glittering with lights, the knights in shining armour, circling the hill and slowly descending to Arthur's Well, where each horse stops to drink the water served to them by their knight. The whole column then returns to the top of the hill and vanishes into the hollow. King Arthur himself has been described as a man of immense stature and dignity. It is recorded that one of those who saw the column of knights descending once picked up a silver horseshoe shed by one of the horses.

Sometimes on wild and stormy nights the king and his hounds have also been seen and heard crossing the causeway named after him. Even now that the actual palace of the king has disappeared the legend lives in the names of the surrounding villages of North and South Cadbury, West Camel and Queens Camel divided by the little river Cam. On the banks of this river the terrible last battle took place between King Arthur and Mordred, the knight who had betrayed him. Mordred was killed and King Arthur severely wounded, his body carried to the barge that bore him to the Isle of Avalon nearby at Glastonbury, where he was buried beside the faithless Guinivere, his wife. Cornwall has its own version of the Arthurian legend and both are beautiful and immortal.

For centuries the monks of Glastonbury Abbey believed deeply in the legend of the king. Then in 1184 a raging fire broke out in the Abbey destroying most of its buildings and relics. The monks travelled miles for funds; after many years their skill and determination enabled them to rebuild it. Five years later they claimed to have discovered King Arthur's grave. They had been inspired in their search by King Henry II, who had once been told by a Welsh bard that the king had been buried so deep that no Saxon would ever find him. When the monks began to excavate they first found a stone, then a red cross with letters which translated read: 'Here lies buried the renowned King Arthur and Guinivere his wife in the Isle of Avalon'. Deeper still they found a huge coffin made from a hollow oak trunk, containing the bones of a strong and extraordinarily large-boned man of great stature. At the other end of the coffin lay a woman's skull, encircled by a yellow tress of hair which still retained its colour and its freshness but crumbled to dust before the eyes of the wondering monks. They had at last proved their belief and faith to an unbelieving world.

GHOSTS AND GARDENS

Gaulden Manor, in Tolland near Taunton, may be difficult to find, but the reward of discovering it for the first time makes any amount of trouble worth while. It stands in some of the most beautiful Somerset countryside between the Quantocks and the Brendon Hills, and has remained virtually unchanged since Plantagenet times, when King John gave Gaulden-in-Tolland with all its lands, rents and privileges to Stavordale Priory in Taunton. It was held by the Priory until the Dissolution of the Monasteries by Henry VIII. During this time the Augustinian Prior of Taunton Priory used to come and collect the rents due to him from what was known as the grange, or small religious house or monastery. One story claims that many monks were buried in one of the gardens known as the Monks' Garden, in which there is a fish pond – always indicating the presence of monks. It is a most peaceful garden, as are the Secret Garden, the Elizabethan Herb Garden and the Bishop's Garden, all created and loved by Mr and Mrs Le Gendre Starkie.

It is not surprising that the manor itself has various ghosts, and these have been accepted by the owners as friendly ones, though they are never actually seen; heavy footsteps are heard on the main staircase and loud knocks on the bedroom door early in the morning. A former housekeeper also heard footsteps in the passages and on the stairs.

Legends tell of secret passages from the manor to Wiveliscombe and to Grove Farm, said to have been a nunnery. These may have been established during the time that James Turberville, Bishop of Exeter, was in refuge here. 'Bloody' Queen Mary had created him the Bishop of Exeter, but as a Catholic he had refused to take the oath of supremacy demanded by the Protestant Queen Elizabeth I, and had been imprisoned in the Tower of London in 1559. Released four years later on condition that he placed himself under the care and watchful eye of the Bishop of London, he appears to have gone into retreat in Gaulden Manor two years later. Fuller in his *Worthies of England* describes him: 'He was a gentleman born and of a good house very gentle and courteous. He carries something of trouble in his name though nothing but mildness and meekness in his nature, the privacy of whose life caused the obscurity of his death.' His place of death is unknown.

Although Bere Regis in Dorset is the ancient family home of the great Norman Turberville family, James Turberville's soul lives on in the superb plaster frieze of the Great Hall of Gaulden Manor. A masterpiece dated circa 1570, this impressive work depicts his religious beliefs and details of his life in images such as the Tower of London and the Scales of Justice, angels and cherubs, David with his harp and the Angel of Judgment. A magnificent 16th-century screen divides the room from the Chapel where there is another frieze, reflecting the peace and tranquillity left by the Bishop. Both are seen by many thousands of visitors. There is no record of his ghost haunting the manor, but the coach of the Turberville family has been seen, a heavy wooden structure drawn by four horses, which travelled about the country from the family home in Bere Regis, Dorset. It has been mentioned in other counties and was reputed to call when one of the family was about to die, as a warning of death.

Brockley Court

That outstanding writer of ghost stories, ghost lore and ghost history, Christina Hole, has written a great deal about the phenomenum of the spectral coach in her book *Haunted England,* and has uncovered countless tales of phantom coaches driven by headless drivers, or drivers carrying headless passengers, or simply a phantom coach without driver or passenger. She writes: 'There is scarcely a road in England along which the spectral coach has not trundled at some time or another. Sometimes it comes to fetch away the dying, sometimes the already dead use it in their perambulations about the roads and fields of their old home.' She has also given examples in her book of coaches turning up as a warning of death to those they visit.

Given the peaceful atmosphere of the Chapel and Great Hall it came as a shock to the author and his wife on a visit to the house, when another visitor to the chapel told us that a friend of his had seen the ghosts of three bloodstained Cavaliers there, and as a result never wanted to see the Chapel again. These ghosts are said to haunt other parts of the manor and have reputedly been seen by other visitors, notably at the head of the stairs. As one of the battles of the Civil Wars was fought nearby, and Cromwell occupied part of the manor for a short time, it is quite possible that the three Cavaliers were killed by the roundheads at this time.

It is comforting to think that another, more peaceful ghost has been seen sitting near the fireplace in the Great Hall, perhaps enjoying the peace of the frieze above. Upstairs is a more sinister room, small and empty, which the previous owner kept locked for the twenty years he lived there (as he told the present owner), as he was sure it was haunted.

Many people have said that this is the most haunted house in Somerset, which seems a quite ridiculous claim. One has only one wish and desire as one leaves Gaulden Manor, and that is to return again soon.

A VERY DANGEROUS GHOST

In ghost history the very worst ghosts are the Poltergeists who are bent on driving owners out of their houses. It is not always clear whether they work individually or in groups, but they are always dangerous. In the case of the Somerset ghost of Brockley Court the ghost is an individual who finally drove his own family from the home they had occupied for centuries. I owe my thanks to the

Society for Psychical Research, for the hand-written documents containing the full story of the ghost, which terrorised one member of the family to such an extent that a Member of the Society personally made a full investigation of the case for their records.

Brockley village, between Bristol airport and Clevedon, had quite a few 'supposed' but not authentic ghosts flitting about the cottages of Brockley Combe and the neighbourhood. Brockley Court is a splendid manor house which belonged to the Smyth-Pigott family and was bought in 1661 by the Right Honorable Thomas Pigott. Nothing of a supernatural nature seems to have been recorded in the house until three centuries later, when on the 23 August 1900 John Smyth-Pigott gave a meticulously detailed account of his first sight of a ghost, to a Member of the Psychical Research Society to whom he had appealed for help.

He had been reading in bed before sleeping as he always did wherever he was staying, when something unusual made him look up from his book, to see in astonishment a figure standing by the door leading into the Arch Room. A counterpane thrown over the bed rail at the bottom prevented him from seeing more than the upper part of the body, which held its hands stretched out in an imploring preventive gesture with the palms downwards, without moving. Then, advancing around and passing the bed it disappeared through the closed door into the passage. It was so near to him that he could see the whole figure, which was dressed in a dark material with a white choker of lace at the neck and what looked like a small rapier at its left side. It was only a little later that he realised that it was the figure of his great-great-great-uncle John Pigott, whose portrait was in the house. He felt convinced of this by the white choker and the hair brushed back over a wide forehead. The face of the figure, however, was vacant and expressionless.

More astonished than alarmed, John Smyth-Pigott kept the candles burning and passed a sleepless night. He told his uncle next morning of the apparition, and he ridiculed the story until his nephew mentioned its resemblance to the portrait. That night John slept in the Green Room once again. He was uneasy but not nervous, and did not expect for one moment that the figure would appear again. It was about eleven o'clock when he began to undress, and as he was taking off his tie he felt there was something behind him. Turning suddenly, he saw it was the figure again, this time moving towards the door leading to the passage, through which it vanished, though the door was not open. Everything happened so swiftly that he had no time to notice details of the figure as before. He rushed at once towards his uncle's room, and meeting him at the end of the passage he told his uncle that he had just seen the ghost. Astonishingly he was not mocked again; instead his uncle told him that he had also seen the ghost.

From that time they both slept in his uncle's room, keeping the ghost secret from the servants and the rest of the family, although his brother Bernard experienced a visitation – which will be related later. About a fortnight later Jack (as he was known in the family) was lying in bed on a sofa at the foot of his uncle's bed, when he felt himself being lifted from a sleeping position to a rising upright one, by what must have been a very strong man, who seemed to be grasping at the lappets of his nightdress. After a few seconds he was released from its hold, and his body fell back on his pillow. Now fully awake, he immediately saw the figure. In the darkness of the room he first became conscious of dark eyes looking at him and realized that the figure was luminous, white, not blue, and was either kneeling or sitting by his bed. It was again only half the figure that he saw, and it remained for almost a minute staring at him. What he did notice was the mouth; it was ugly, the corners drooped. Then the figure seemed to melt away rather than move suddenly.

Yet another visitation has been graphically described by Mr Smyth-Pigott:

> I was in the Arch Room in bed reading, as was also my uncle. My bed, a small one, stood at the end of my uncle's large bed. There were at least 2 candles burning and probably three. We were both wide awake, only having been in bed some 5 minutes. I suddenly heard my uncle's book close with a bang. I sat up to look over on to his bed, and saw his arms stretched out in front of him with the hands clenched. He was struggling and trying to draw himself back. Quite suddenly he fell out of bed head foremost on to the floor, with his legs up in the air quite close to my bed. I then saw him being dragged along the floor round the projecting closet towards the door leading into the passage. He was being pulled on his stomach along the floor by the wrists – or apparently by the wrists, as his arms were in the air above his head. Hardly knowing what I was doing I rushed out of the door that leads through the powder closet and green room into the passage. Arrived in the passage I saw that the other door, towards which my uncle had been dragged was shut so I rushed back into the Arch Room where I found my uncle lying on the floor by the door in exhaust-

ed condition. I raised him up and got him back to bed. He then and there said that he had seen the figure standing by one of the pillars, which is close to the head of my bed; that after standing there for a few moments, it came forward, seized him by the wrists, and then dragged him in the manner described. He saw the figure the whole time, and it kept its eyes fixed on him. After a few minutes we both went downstairs to fetch a priest, Father Roake, who was staying in the house. He came up and blessed the room – after which we went to bed again, leaving our candles burning. About an hour later, neither of us having slept, the figure suddenly appeared at the foot of my bed by another pillar. When my uncle was dragged out of bed I saw no figure, but we both saw it now at the same time and in the same place. My uncle came down to the end of his bed and we caught hold of each other's hand and began to talk to the ghost. We asked it several questions. I asked it why it came several times. But the ghost did not reply to any question, except when I asked 'Why are you here?' It replied: 'This is my home.' My uncle heard nothing, but I heard the words spoken clearly in a deep and expressionless voice. A second or two after speaking it disappeared.

Mr Smyth-Pigott, in an earlier part of the interview he gave, stated that the appearances of the ghost were so frequent that he could not detach them one from another with sufficient accuracy. He said:

> I used to wake up to find the face only within sometimes a yard or less of my own face – sometimes the full figure by my bedside. Sometimes while I was watching the face, it would recede and then disappear. No sound ever accompanied the appearances. The features appeared the same on all occasions. It was a malicious, horrible face. The last occasion on which I saw the figure during my summer stay at Brockley Court was 3 or 4 days before we left, which we did on 23 September.

Mr Bernard Smyth-Pigott was also consulted about his own experiences, and they too were extremely frightening. He had been told about the ghost by his brother; two days later he was sleeping in the schoolroom with his younger brother Rushcombe. He awoke about 1.30 feeling ill, getting up and turning into the passage he saw 'John' standing by the Green Room door, dressed as in the family portrait. His description of the ghost was the same as his brother Jack's had been, but this time the spectre seemed to be talking, though no sounds came. Bernard was petrified. The candle fell out of the candlestick in his hand and he bolted back to his bedroom. Next morning he went away to make a visit to some friends.

Some six or seven days later Bernard returned, sleeping in the same bedroom as before, this time with his uncle for companion. Being nervous, he kept waking, there being a little light in the room from bright moonlight coming through the shutters. About a minute before he saw the ghost he found himself bathed in perspiration and tingling all over. It came *through* the cupboard and to the foot of his uncle's bed, then disappeared *through* the door. He woke his uncle and they opened the door but nothing was there. He saw nothing further for a week and then experienced the same sensations before seeing the white figure. This time, in full moonlight, he was able to see the piercing bright eyes though not the lower part of the face.

Yet in spite of all that had happened the family assembled in December for Christmas. This time Mr John Smyth-Pigott had brought with him a Mr Marius Bode of Keble College, Oxford, who was extremely anxious to see the ghost. They were sleeping in the Arch Room, his friend in the larger bed, he in the smaller. He was awakened by being raised in bed and found the ghost behind the head of his bed. It moved round to Bode's bed and disappeared into the wall. Bode was still sleeping and so unfortunately missed what he had come to see. This must have been a great disappointment as he could have been a valuable witness outside the family to what was surely a series of almost unbelievable experiences. Had not the member of the Psychical Research Society meticulously documented his expert investigation into this most frightening of ghost stories, nobody could possibly have believed the facts faithfully recorded.

'This is my home' the ghost had said; but the reason for that statement will never be known and must remain an unsolved mystery, as so many ghost stories have been. For a very long time before things reached such a crisis in Brockley Court its reputation as a haunted house had been widely known, even beyond the village, so that it became almost impossible to persuade servants to work there.

The most pleasant memorial to the Smyth-Pigott family is in the little adjoining church of St Nicholas, with its Norman door, 13th-century windows, box pews and three hatchments. The family spent a great deal of money during the 18th century on the church, and whether or not by design so that their presence should be permanently felt, their pew remains opposite the pulpit. It is a large room containing period chairs and a huge, comfortable armchair, all in front of a fireplace, to ensure a good sleep during the three hour sermons given in those times. The key to the church can be obtained from their old home, which has now been converted into a residential home for elderly people, which may well have given the greatest pleasure to the family.

ONE NIGHT OF TERROR

A documented ghost story involving sacrilege in a church, an unseen but often-heard ghost, robbery, body-snatchers, and a greedy sexton, took place four centuries ago in Kentsford Farm and at St Decuman's church near Watchet in Somerset. The mystery of it all might have been forgotten, but it was revived within the last thirty years when the occupants of Kentsford Farm repeatedly heard tapping on the windows as if someone were trying to get in, though whoever it was remains unknown. The house was the original manor house of the Wyndham family, who had bought it in the early sixteenth century from the Luttrell family of Dunster Castle in Somerset. In 1588, the year of the Armada, John Wyndham married Florence Wadham, and both went to live in the beautiful manor house, never knowing what was going to happen to the young wife.

The manor house was divided by fields from the church, one of the largest in the county, built upon a hill near the little town of Watchet. It had its own remarkable legend for its founder was Saint Decuman who, like so many other saints, came from Ireland to Britain, using either a raft or a hurdle to land somewhere in Wales. He was accompanied by a cow 'joining him of her own wish in order that her milk might keep him from starvation'. He landed later in the little port of Watchet and became a hermit at a place where he had soon decided he would found his church. The people, however, found his presence unwelcome, for unknown reasons, and so they beheaded him. St Decuman, however, immediately picked up his head, washed the blood away in a stream and placed it back on his neck again before departing from his hermitage to cross the channel again, probably to Brittany.

When the church came to be built it was naturally named after him. It is filled with brasses, monuments and tombs to generations of the Wyndham family, most of which are in the Wyndham Chapel. There, after a sad short marriage, Florence Wyndham's body was placed in the family vault. The 'illness' from which she is supposed to have died was not uncommon in those days. It was probably what would now be called a cataleptic trance, and though rare it is not unknown. Not a few people were believed to have died suddenly and were put in their coffins as soon as possible and buried. The sexton of the church at that time was a man named Attewell, who naturally assisted at the funeral and had seen her in her coffin. He also knew her to be a rich lady and had noticed what she was wearing on her fingers as she lay in her coffin before it was screwed down and taken to the church for burial.

That same night he left his house, crossed the fields and ascended the hill to enter the church with his own key. Lighting a lantern he entered the vault, where Florence's coffin lay beneath that of Sir John Wyndham and his wife Elizabeth. Hurriedly he prized open the coffin lid and saw at once the jewellery she wore on her neck and on the fingers of her clasped hands. He started on the fingers, struggling to shift the rings from them, even using his knife to do so. All was going well when suddenly his knife slipped into his own finger and blood flowed. In a panic he still tried to remove two more rings. Already alarmed at what had happened he was terrified when Florence suddenly moved; her eyes opened, and she sat up, staring at him in astonishment and demanding what he was doing with her ringed fingers. In his horror, kicking over the lantern in his haste, the robber fled from the church, scared out of his wits by the sight of what he thought was a spectre rising from her grave in her white shroud. She herself was hot pursuit after what she knew must be a body-snatcher. She had already picked up the lantern to light up the church and the darkness outside as she followed the thief through the door and outside into the night.

There are two accounts of what happened to Attewell. One was that he rushed to the sea and drowned himself; according to the other version he reached his house and collapsed, sending for the rector next morning to hear what had happened. His story was that he had been disturbed by a light near the church, and going to see what was happening was set upon by two body-snatchers. They had demanded his keys and forced him to open the door and lead them to the Wyndham vault where they knew a rich lady had been buried. The ruffians had then ordered him to cut the rings from the fingers of the corpse and when he had refused they had threatened to kill him. In terror he had set about the deed but had cut his finger in the process, showing the rector his finger and telling him that proof of his story was the blood that must still be on part of the coffin or the stone floor. Having told his story he died that same evening.

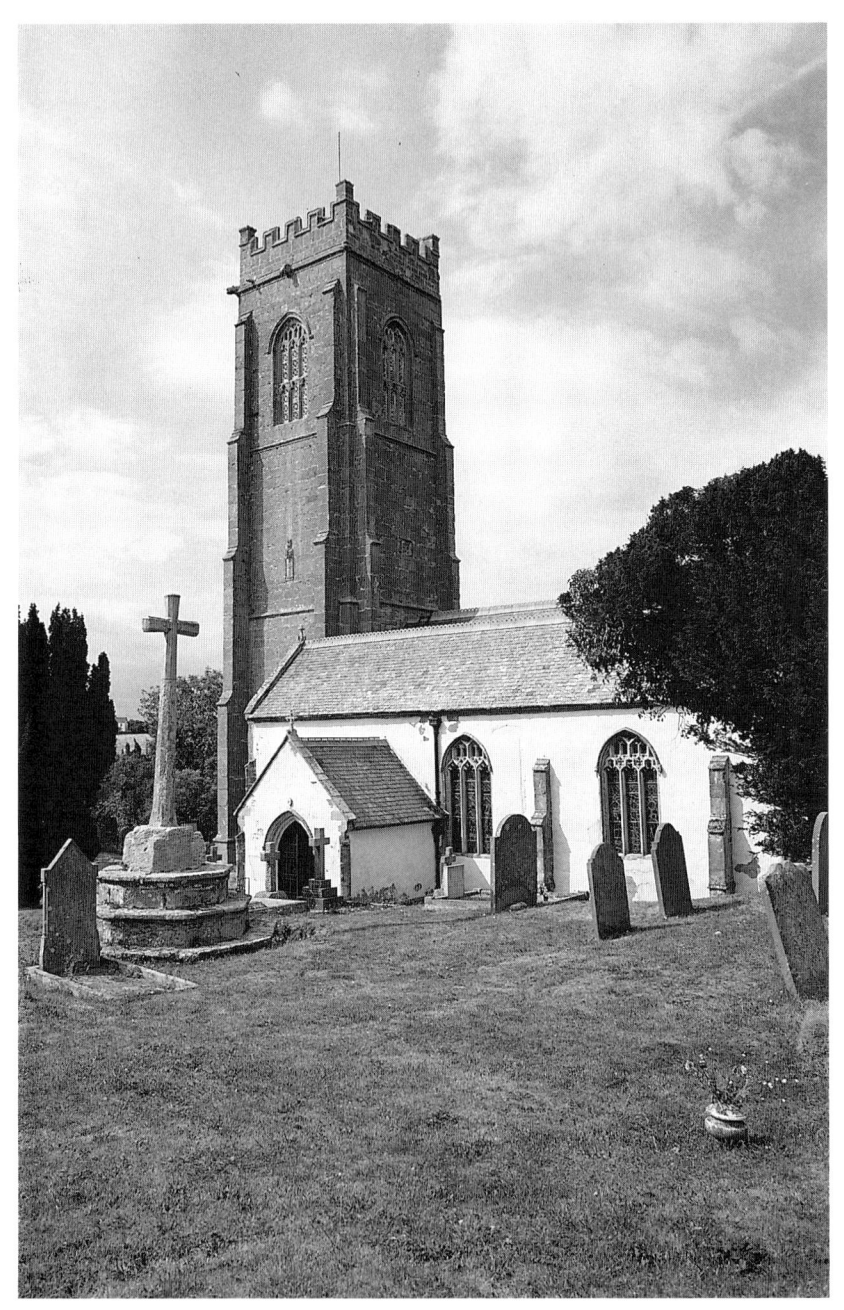

St Decuman's Church, Watchet

Florence Wyndham, however, having lost sight of Attewell, made back across the fields to her home, but despite her tapping on the windows and beating on the door to get in she had no response other than the barking of the dog. The servants, frightened out of their lives by the sounds, made no move to open the door. Finally her husband, alerted no doubt by the servants, dared to open the door to see his wife, shivering as she almost collapsed, huddled in her white grave shroud and unable to say a word. In spite of her horrific experience she later bore a son, who was knighted. She also had eight more children and lived to a great age before being re-buried in the family vault in the church of St Decuman. The ghost of Florence Wyndham has never been seen, but only heard tapping on the windows at certain times of the year.

The 14th-century gate to Salisbury Cathedral Close

WILTSHIRE

THE DEMON DRUMMER OF TEDWORTH

The case of the Demon Drummer of Tedworth is probably the most famous in the history of poltergeists. It is also significant as the identity of the poltergeist should have been recognised throughout the nerve-racking manifestations, certainly by the owner of the house, who was in fact the instigator of all the years of torment. Yet John Mompesson, a magistrate of high repute, seemed not to have understood the nature of the manifestations until the very last, allowing ceaseless terror to himself, his wife and children, and a considerable number of servants.

On a day in mid-March 1661 he went to Ludgershall, not far away from Tedworth, where he lived, to attend to his court duties. He was surprised, indeed disturbed by the continual beating of a drum up and down the street, as this usually proclaimed news of importance to the town. He at once sent for the Bailiff for an explanation and was even more surprised when he was told that the drummer had been beating his drum throughout the past few days. His name was William Drury, an idle fellow, who when questioned by the Bailiff as to his reason for disturbing the peace, replied that he had every right to so as he had a warrant. This warrant seemed to be in order, so the Bailiff dismissed him with a warning.

Mompesson, not happy about this, demanded that the drummer should be brought to him for questioning. Drury was at once brought before him, and when asked for his warrant produced it. It was signed by Sir William Cawley and Colonel Ayliffe, both personally known to Mompesson who at once recognised that the signatures were forged. Drury told him he had been a regimental drummer in one of Cromwell's regiments, and begged Mompesson not to make him take off his drum. He was then charged with disturbance of the peace, vagrancy, and false documents and was taken to the Justice of the Peace for punishment. His drum would be retained meanwhile and Drury, in spite of earnest pleading, was led away by the constable, who, it seems, was so sorry for the man's earnest pleas that he let him go free.

It was then that the real trouble began. Mompesson returned to his house with the drum to find his wife almost out of her mind with fright, assuring him that thieves had been in the house, making so much noise that the house was 'like to have been broken up'. Mompesson at once armed himself with pistols and searched the house, but found nothing and believed his wife to have imagined it all. It was not long before he himself had his first fright, hearing the banging of door after door as he entered rooms, with heavy drumming somewhere in the house becoming louder and louder, particularly during the night. Mrs Mompesson was expecting a child at any moment, and it was born that night after a terrifying series of noises with drumming everywhere in the house. This mercifully passed and there was peace and quiet for three weeks before it started all over again.

On the 5th November 1662 'it made a mighty noise' as the Reverend Joseph Glanvil wrote in his Journal *Sadducismus Triumphatus*, one of the most carefully documented journals in the history of poltergeists. He was called to the house by Mompesson and became witness to almost every detail he described. On that November night the children were so frightened that a servant went to their room; there he saw a board moving which he took hold of, but it was pulled from him and a tug of war began. Mompesson, disturbed by the noise and screams of the children told his servant to stop his antics. He also called in Mr Cragg, a Minister, and begged him to say prayers for the safety of his house and family. Strangely enough the 'Spirit' departed until the prayers were finished and then resumed its noise, 'even throwing a bed-staff at the Minister, which hit him on the leg'. All this was witnessed by a number of neighbours who had heard the noise outside and come into the house to see what was happening.

It seemed then that the prevailing noise was the steady beating of a drum 'beating Roundheads and Cuckolds Tattoo', for an hour or more as if calling the Guard. It seems incredible that Mompesson had not even the slightest suspicion that this could be the work of magic, by the Drummer beating his drum. After all the drum was still in the house. Towards the end of December the noise was so bad that neighbours were deeply concerned. Strangely enough no dogs barked. The drumming began to lessen and was replaced by the sound of jingling money. One neighbour told Glanvil that it was probably the work of fairies, and might mean they were making amends to the Mompessons for what they had done. Not even Christmas was spared by the spirit, for one of the children was hit on the ankle as he lay in bed. On Christmas day a gentlewoman of the house had her clothes thrown all over the room and her Bible into the ashes. Glanvil records: 'Mr Mompesson took it up and observed that it lay open at the third chapter of St Mark, where there is mention of the unclean spirits falling down before our saviour, and of his giving power to the twelve to cast out devils, and of the scribe's opinion that he cast them out through Beelzebub.'

Glanvil's own manservant was terrified by the sight of one of his master's horses in the stable 'who looked as if he had been rid all night'. It was one of Glanvil's favourites, and for no known reason it died three days later. The ordeal was endless in the Mompesson household, with noise, sleepless nights, knockings, bed-clothes snatched off, sighing and panting noises as if from an unseen animal, and the endless beating of the drum; yet still the children and Mompesson's wife remained in the house. One morning a light was seen in the children's bedroom and a voice heard crying 'a Witch, a Witch,' for more than a hundred times. Again Glanvil writes: 'Mr Mompesson one day seeing something moving in the chimney (as of itself) discharged his pistol into it, after which they found several drops of blood on the hearth, and in divers places of the stairs.'

Finally after some two years of fear and terror came relief, for news came of the drummer, William Drury, who had been arrested on a charge of stealing pigs. He was tried at Salisbury assizes and committed to Gloucester Gaol for stealing. While he was there he had a visit from a Wiltshire man who, when Drury asked him what news he had from there, said he knew of none. The drummer expressed surprise that the man knew nothing of Tedworth and Mr Mompesson who had stolen his drum. 'I have plagued him and he shall never be quiet till he has made me satisfaction for taking away my drum.' The visitor reported this, and Drury was sent to Sarum and sentenced to transportation for life for witchcraft, a sentence which for many was worse than death. Somehow he managed to escape from the sailor who was in charge of taking him to the ship, and was once again at liberty. The noises began all over again at the house of Mr Mompesson. There has never been any explanation of how or when there was final peace in Tedworth, but the poltergeist had certainly ceased by the time Glanvil had published his book nineteen years later in 1682.

In support of the validity of all he wrote and personally experienced Glanvil sums up everything in his final words on the occurrences: 'Mr Mompesson is a Gentleman of whose truth in this account I have not the least ground of suspicion. Now the credit of matters of fact depends much upon the relators who, if they cannot be deceived themselves nor supposed any ways interested to impose on 'thers, ought to be credited. For upon these circumstances all humane faith is grounded, and matter of fact is not capable of any proof besides but that of immediate sensible evidence.'

THE GHOSTS OF LITTLECOTE HOUSE

Five centuries after it first took place, the brutal, callous murder of a mysterious baby in a still-haunted room in Littlecote House has become a legend. Littlecote House, originally Littlecote Manor, is a fine example of Elizabethan architecture. It is in Wiltshire between Ramsbury and Hungerford and is open to the public. A high proportion of the thousands of visitors to the house go there because of the legend of Wild Will Darell, a knight and former owner. Near to the house is a stile known to this day as Darell's Stile. It is haunted by his ghost, for it was there that he was killed when thrown off his horse, both horse and rider having been startled by the sight of the ghost of the murdered child. The fall broke his neck, and he died, the last of his line, three years later.

It was in the year 1575, on a wild and windy night, that the drama began. Mrs Barnes of Great Shefford in Berkshire, a midwife, was rudely awakened from her sleep by a violent knocking on the door of her house. She had had a hard day and had gone to bed early. She could hear the stamp of horses' feet, gruff voices and further violent bangs on her door. As she went downstairs and opened the door she saw two saddled horses and two men, one of whom gruffly told her to get dressed and come with him at once. It was pouring with rain and pitch dark; as she protested she was again ordered to get dressed at once and come out. It was a greater shock when she closed her door and came outside to be ordered to stand still while one of the men blindfolded her. She was then helped on to a horse as pillion to the rider before both horses set off at a gallop.

On arriving at their destination she was helped down and led to a door which had opened in answer to their loud knocking, and a figure took her hand and led her in and up a flight of stairs which she began to count, along a long passage and into a chamber where someone removed her blindfold. She saw at once that it was a richly furnished room in which a four-poster bed stood, where a very beautiful lady lay watching her as she came in. Beside the bed stood a very tall gentleman in a black cloak who watched the lady as she moved with the sudden pains of labour. A great log fire was burning and the room was very hot. The gentleman told Mother Barnes, now quite terrified, that he would come back when the lady was delivered of her child. One account says that the man told her if she succeeded in a safe delivery of the child she would be greatly rewarded. If she failed she would die.

At the cries of the child as it was born the man entered the room and commanded Mother Barnes to hand him the babe. Then, without a word, he snatched the baby and flung it straight into the back of the blazing fire, crushing it with the heel of his boot until it was completely burned to ashes. Mother Barnes, shocked beyond words at this brutal murder, gripped one of the curtains to prevent herself fainting, and managed to keep a piece of the fabric. The man then commanded someone to come in, and again the midwife, still in terror, was blindfolded, taken back along the passage and down the staircase and out to the horses, on one of which she was mounted pillion as before. In silence they rode back to her home where the man helped her off the horse, removed her blindfold, warned her solemnly that she should keep silence if she wanted to go on living, gave her a gold guinea and rode away at a gallop.

Mother Barnes kept her secret for fourteen years and did not make her deposition to Anthony Bridges, a magistrate, until she was on her death bed, when she gave sufficient evidence to cause the arrest and trial of Wild Will Darell of Littlecote House. She had recorded the number of stairs she had taken that led her along a passage to the chamber where the crime was committed; the description of a richly furnished room, a lady in bed she did not know and the gentleman standing by the bedside who threw the babe into the fire, and the damning evidence of the piece of curtain she had torn from the bedside, all identified the place. Every single detail she gave was thus recorded, but three hundred years were to pass before the magistrate's record was proven. The whole story was written by Sir Walter Scott in his novel *Rokeby*, although his version is vague and far from the truth.

For two centuries the chamber was haunted by a frantic woman with dishevelled hair, clutching a baby in her arms, who was seen by many people.

In the year 1879 an important letter was discovered in Longleat, the magnificent home of the Marquis of Bath, by Canon Jackson. It had been sent to Sir John Thynne by Sir Henry Knyvett of Charlton, and was dated 11 January 1575, before the date of Mother Barnes' deposition, beseeching him to urge Mr Benham, then a servant at

Longleat, 'to examine his sister, touching her usage at William Darrell's, the birth of her children, how many they were and what became of them.' He then referred to 'the brute of the murder of one of them increaseth fowely.'

The unsavoury life of Darell was well known in Elizabethan times. He had many mistresses and was known to have incestuous affairs with his sister, who was rumoured to have been the mother of the babe he threw in the fire. Indeed as late as the 19th century there were rumours of his haunting, and an entry in the *Gentleman's Magazine,* 1823 stated: 'In the dusk the country people have often seen in the avenue to the house a coach curiously drawn by six horses, in which are a gentleman and a lady richly dressed, a child of angelic beauty on her lap, but both the gentleman and the lady were headless.'

It was on Mother Barnes' evidence alone that Darell was arrested and went on trial for murder before Sir John Popham, then Attorney General, and was acquitted. Gossip and rumour said that Popham had been bribed by Darell and that both were unscrupulous. The bribe was no less than the vast estate and mansion of Littlecote which passed to Popham three years after the death of Darell in 1589. By a curious irony both of them died while hunting, Darell breaking his neck, Popham drowning in a bottomless well. Popham lives on in legend by his wife's prayers to save his soul and bring it from the well to the church at Wellington near Taunton in Somerset, where he and his wife are buried. To achieve this it had to make one cock's stride a year from Hell to the church. Darrell's ghost is seen holding a burning babe.

In 1843 when General Leyborne-Popham succeeded to Littlecote House, he was pestered by the constant requests of visitors to see the haunted chamber; he burnt the bedcurtains with their piece torn out, the bedstead being disposed of by an auction sale in Dorset in July 1910. But yet again Littlecote became curiously notorious when one of this family's children lay seriously ill, in a room overlooking the entrance to the house guarded by tall iron gates. The child had been so ill that the nurse had sent an express messenger to the parents. She heard the sound of a coach arriving, the gates opening and the bell ringing. When she looked out of the window there was nothing. The child's father, Francis Popham, arrived the next day but the child had died in the night. Later he told the nurse that legend said whenever a child was about to die Wild Darell always came to the house in his chariot.

In 1947 the owners of Littlecote House were Sir Edward and Lady Wills, of the great tobacco firm. One night they both saw the ghost of a distracted tall lady, fair headed and wearing a pink nightdress. As she moved swiftly along the magnificent Long Gallery Sir Edward and Lady Wills both turned to follow her. She was carrying a lighted candle that cast a great shadow over the ceiling. As she reached the door of the room at the end she did something ghosts rarely do: instead of vanishing she actually opened the door and closed it behind her. Sometimes they heard terrifying screams from the haunted chamber and along the Long Gallery.

Guides showing visitors around the house have often seen ghosts. One reported he had definitely seen Mrs Leybourne-Popham, a most beautiful lady according to her portrait. The ghost of a limping figure was constantly seen, who was identified much later as Gerard Lee Bevan who had bought the house. He was a wealthy city financier, and whenever he came down from London he would insolently stop the train to get off at Hungerford station by pulling the communication cord, always paying the fine, which at that time was five pounds. He was a great womaniser, highly successful in the city and chairman of the City Equitable Fire Insurance Company. Early in 1922 the company crashed with debts totalling four million pounds, a huge sum then, leaving millions of shareholders ruined. Bevan escaped to Paris with one of his many women, posing as an artist. He was finally arrested and sentenced to five years penal servitude. On his release he went to Havana where he died. It is difficult to believe that this beautiful house and grounds could be haunted by any ghost, let alone the fearful ghost of Wild Will Darell, yet even today the majority of visitors are those who have read about him and his brutal character.

GHOSTS GALORE IN LONGLEAT

Of all the stately homes of England probably none has been more haunted than Longleat in Wiltshire, home of the Marquess of Bath, the first to have opened its house to the public. Its safari park with the famous Longleat Lions, the great lake and the gardens have attracted millions of people there. They come and they go, but the ghosts of Longleat have been there throughout its long history. They are in the Stable Courtyard, Bishop Ken's Library, the Red Library, and the most mysterious, in one of the corridors known as the Green Lady's Walk.

It is not surprising that there is a ghost of Sir John Thynne, the first of the line to build the great mansion and known as 'The Builder'. All his first efforts were destroyed by fire and in the year 1567 he began all over again. Queen Elizabeth I was curious to see the place and Sir John finally had to give in to welcoming her there on one of her Progresses, although the cost of her visits was enormous and had bankrupted quite a few of her hosts. He died before Longleat was completed but part of it was his beloved Red Library of which he was proud. It is there that he has been seen so many times and accepted as a very kindly ghost.

Curiously there was a second library known as Bishop Ken's Library. This is supposed to have been haunted quite regularly by the Bishop himself at midnight on the anniversary of his death in 1711. In that fine library he wrote many of his hymns and dedicated his Divine Poems to Viscount Weymouth. He might well have ended his clerical career earlier than he did for when he was at Winchester he refused to allow Nell Gwynne to have lodgings in the cathedral close. When Charles II was informed of this he made no comment, indeed he seemed indifferent. Later, however, when the bishopric of Bath and Wells fell vacant the king asked 'Where is that good little man who refused his lodging to poor Nell?' and gave him the appointment. This was a valuable preferment because Longleat was in his diocese, and Viscount Weymouth of Longleat had been his closest friend since their Oxford days. Whenever he had time, and after his retirement, the gentle bishop spent every available hour in the library. No wonder his spirit returned so often there.

There are many ghosts at Longleat, including one in a linen cupboard, another in the Stable Courtyard, and another who has often been seen and heard knocking on the door of one of the bedrooms and in the corridor. But the strangest one of all, and the most frightening, is the ghost in the corridor known as The Green Lady's Walk. In her splendid little book on Longleat the Marchioness of Bath gives a short account of the origin of the ghost of the Green Lady, who was the second wife of the second Viscount Weymouth. She was the very beautiful Lady Louisa Cartaret, admired by everybody who saw her. Sarah, Duchess of Marlborough, in one of her letters expressed her surprise that she should have married such a man.

The second Viscount Weymouth was indeed an odd man and was very unpopular in the district. He did not live long at Longleat, for when his step-father Lord Lansdowne came to visit he stayed so long that the Viscount moved out of the mansion into a cottage, and he

Longleat

never returned to the house. Apparently he scoffed at tradition, ostentatious wealth and large mansions. His second marriage turned out to be as miserable as his first, and it was not surprising that the beautiful Louisa met a young man and fell in love. As it was impossible for them to meet in the house where she and her husband lived, they planned to meet in Longleat, since Lord Weymouth had never returned there. One day the Viscount, either because he had become suspicious or for some other reason, entered Longleat and found the two together in a room at the top of the house. A duel was fought between the two men and the lover was killed. This was in the early eighteenth century. The passage where the duel is thought to have taken place has been haunted ever since by the ghost of Lady Louisa Cartaret and known as The Green Lady's Walk.

In the early twentieth century the fifth Marquess of Bath had central heating installed in the house. During this work a body was dis-

Lady Louisa Cartaret, Longleat's 'Green Lady'

covered under the floor in one of the cellars. It was of a man wearing jackboots, and as soon as the body was exposed it crumbled to dust. Curiously enough the fifth Marchioness, who wrote the book about Longleat, was living there at the time the body was found. She was herself psychic and one day in 1916 she was sitting at the window when she saw five swans flying very low above the great lake, heading for the house. Suddenly one of them flew away from the others and disappeared into the distance. She told her family that this was a bad omen, for there was a legend that should one swan ever fly away and not return, it meant that one of the family would die. She at once feared for the life of her son, Viscount Weymouth, who was fighting in France in World War I. The very next day a telegram was brought to her announcing his death in action.

Later still she asked one day why all the dust sheets were over the furniture and the floor in the Hall, but no one understood what she was talking about. The significance of the vision was revealed when fire broke out in the roof, severely damaging it so that workmen had to go up to do repairs, first covering everything in the magnificent Hall to prevent damage. She must have felt at home with all the other ghosts in her beautiful mansion.

THE REMORSEFUL GHOST

In the history of ghosts it is probably true to say that any who return do so for a purpose. It may be sorrow at leaving their home, to comfort those left behind, or even out of revenge and to create fear and terror, as may be the case with poltergeists. It is refreshing to hear of a ghost who has returned out of remorse and to clear its conscience for something done in its previous life. This is the story of Edward Avon, who died in Marlborough in May 1674. His ghost was driven by his conscience to repay a debt and to confess a crime.

The authentication of this narrative was published in 1854 by James Waylen in *A History of Marlborough,* in which a statement was made by Edward Avon's son-in-law, Thomas Goddard, a weaver. Goddard gave his deposition before the Town Clerk, the Rector of St Peter's church and others, describing his encounter with the ghost on 11 November 1674. This was on the very day he saw the apparition. He said that as early as nine o'clock that morning on his way to Ogbourn he had reached a stile on the highway, when suddenly he saw the ghost, whom he recognised as his father-in-law Edward Avon. There was no doubt about this: he was wearing the same clothes, hat, gloves, shoes as he always wore, and was leaning against the stile facing Goddard. 'I am the man you were thinking of,' he said. 'I am Edward Avon, your father-in-law. Come near to me. I will do you no harm.'

He then enquired quite naturally about various members of the family, his son William a shoemaker and Mary his daughter, who was Goddard's wife. He then asked about Mr Taylor who had married Sarah, Avon's other daughter. Taylor had died at Michaelmas. Then suddenly the ghost held out his hand in which Goddard saw some twenty or thirty silver shillings glittering. Suddenly in a loud voice he said 'Take this money and send it to Sarah. Mary (meaning Goddard's wife) is troubled for me but tell her I have received mercy contrary to my deserts.' When Goddard refused to take the money Avon said 'I see you are afraid, so I will see you another time,' and vanished. Goddard went over the stile on his way.

The next night the ghost reappeared at about seven o'clock, still in the same clothes, looking at him through his shop window but saying nothing. Then it vanished as before. The next night it came again as Goddard was in his back premises and holding a lighted candle. But this time Goddard, in great fear, rushed past the ghost and into his house. The night after that, as Goddard was riding home across the fields from Chilton, he saw what looked like a hare that caused his horse to throw him to the ground. As soon as he had recovered from his shock the ghost appeared again, about eight feet in front of him, and still in the same clothes. Once again he spoke in a very loud commanding voice, saying: 'You have stayed long, Thomas. Bid William Avon take the sword that he had of me, which is now in his house, and carry it to the wood as we go to Alton, to the upper end of the wood by the wayside, for with that sword I did wrong about thirty years ago and he has never prospered since he had that sword. And bid William Avon give his sister Sarah twenty shillings of the money he had of me. And do you talk with Edward Lawrence, for I borrowed twenty shillings of him several years ago and did say I had paid him but I did not and I desire you to pay him out of the money which you had from James Elliot a baker…'

After giving details of several more small debts he desired to be paid, the apparition vanished.

Goddard said he saw no more of the ghost at that time, but strangely moved with compassion by the spirit's anxiety to repay his debts, he decided to do everything he could to help. First he would deal with the sword, and on the Mayor's orders he went with

William, who carried the sword, the following morning at nine o'clock to the wood. Suddenly the ghost appeared and again in a loud voice said: 'Thomas, take up the sword and follow me' and all three moved deeper into the wood until they reached a copse, where the ghost stopped and turned. Goddard saw that what appeared to be a brown dog stood beside the apparition. It then turned again to speak to Goddard, the mastiff still beside him, saying, 'I have a commission not to touch you.' Taking the sword from Goddard he pointed it downwards to a spot in the copse, at the same time speaking clearly. 'In this place lies buried the body of him which I murdered in the year 1635, which is now rotten and turned to dust.' Goddard then asked him why he had committed this crime, and what it had to do with him. The ghost answered: 'This is that the world may know that I murdered a man and buried him in this place in the year 1635.' Suddenly the ghost laid down the sword and vanished. Goddard never saw him again. This astonishing story of the repentant ghost was told before important witnesses and documented, becoming an important part of local history.

BIBLIOGRAPHY

Automobile Association	*Country Towns and Villages of Britain*, 1985
Aubrey, J.	*Miscellanies*, 1696
	Brief Lives, 1949
Baring-Gould, S.	*Cornish Characters and Strange Events*, 1935
Braddock, J.	*Haunted Houses*, 1986
Briggs, K.M. & Tongue, R.L.	*Folktales of England*
Brooks, J.	*Railway Ghosts*
Collinson, J.	*History of Somerset*, 1791
Colton, Rev. C.	*Narrative of the Sampford Ghost*
Crowe, C.	*The Night Side of Nature*, 1848
Curtis, C.	*Sedgemoor and the Bloody Assizes*, 1930
Dale, Owen E.	*Footfalls on the Boundary of Another World*, 1859
Day, J.W.	*A Ghost-hunter's Guide Book*, 1956
Ellis, S.M.	*Short stories and legends of Berry Pomeroy Castle*
Fox, A.	*King Monmouth*, 1902
Fuller	*Worthies of England*
Halifax, Viscount.	*Lord Halifax's Ghost Book*, 1936
Hall, T.H.	*New Lights on Old Ghosts*, 1965
Hanning, P.	*Dictionary of Ghosts*, 1982
Harper, G.C.	*Haunted Houses*, 1924
Hole, C.	*Haunted England*, 1940
Hunt, R.	*Popular Romances of the West of England*
Jarvis	*Accredited Ghost Stories*, 1823
Johnson, W.	*Folk Memory*, 1908
Lawrence, B.	*Somerset Legends*
Legg, R.	*A Guide to Dorset Ghosts*
Maple, E.	*The Realm of Ghosts*, 1964
Marc, A.	*Haunted Castles*
Norman, D.	*The Stately Ghosts of England*, 1963
O'Donnell, E.	*Haunted Britain (third impression)*
	Ghost Short Stories, 1909
Page, M.	*The Battle of Sedgemoor*, 1930
Palmer, K.	*The Folklore of Somerset*
Poole, K.B.	*Ghosts of Wessex*, 1976
Powley, E.B.	*Official Guide of Berry Pomeroy Castle*

Price, H.	*Poltergeists Over England*
Roy, C.	*Ghosts and Legends*, 1975
Russell, E.	*Ghosts*, 1975
Sergeant, P.W.	*Historic British Ghosts*
Sitwell, S.	*Poltergeists*, 1940
Tongue, R.L.	*Folklore of Somerset*
Turner, J.	*Ghosts of the South West*, 1973
Underwood, P.A.	*A Gazetter of British Ghosts*, 1971
	West Country Hauntings, 1986

Publications covering counties in this book are:
The King's England: Arthur Mee
Highways and Byways: various authors
The Buildings of England: (ed.) Nikolaus Pevsner
Gentleman's Magazine
Notes and Queries

Also:
Society for Psychical Research
Local historical societies, field clubs, county histories, regional journals and magazines.

INDEX

All Saints Vicarage 12
All The Year Round 13
Altarnun 35
Arthurian Ghosts 96
Assembly Rooms 15
Athelhampton Hall 68, 71
Avon 9
Avon, Edward 121

Barberi, Dominic 86
Baring-Gould, Sabine 52
Bath 15
Battiscombe, Christopher 82
Beaminster 69, 71, 82
Beast of the Moors, the 64
Bere Regis 99
Berepper 30
Berkeley Castle 84, 87, 88
Berry Pomeroy Castle 7, 60, 63
Bettiscombe Manor House 77, 78
Bishop's Nympton 66
Bodmin Moor 27, 40, 41, 66
Botathan House 35
Bovill, John 31
Bridges, Anthony 115
Bristol 9
Bristol Times, the 12
Broadrep, Colonel 70
Brockley Court 100, 101
Broome, Theophilus 93

Cadbury Castle 96
Cartaret, Lady Louisa 119, 120
Case, Sally 55
Chambercombe Manor 47, 49, 50
Chave, John 54
Chilton Cantelo Farmhouse 92, 93
Churchill, Sir Winston 7
Clifton Down 9

Colton, Caleb 55
Cornwall 21, 66

Daniel, John 69
Darell, William 114
Dartmoor 65
Davidstow 40, 43, 44
Devon 47
Dew Pond 52
Dingley, Dorothy 35, 38
Dockacre House 25
Dodington, George 75
Doggett, William 76
Dorchester 79
Dorset 69
Dozmary Pool 28
Drury, William 111, 113
Dymond, Charlotte 40, 42

Eastbury 75
Ellingham 82
Exmoor 64, 65

Farquhar, Dr Walter 61

Galford 52
Garrick's Head Hotel, the 8, 15, 18
Gaulden Manor 98
Gaveston, Piers 90
Giles, Henry 94
Glanvil, Joseph 112
Glastonbury Abbey 98
Glastonbury Tor 97
Gloucestershire 85
Goddard, Thomas 121
Good, Thomas 44
Gorges family 47
Green Lady's Walk, the 119
Grey Lady, the 16, 74

126

Gurney, Thomas 90
Gwynne, Nell 118

Hanging Tree, the 81
Hardy, Thomas 71, 73
Harper, Charles 58
Heddon Oak, the 81
Herle, Nicholas and Elizabeth 26
Hewling, William 82
Higher Downgate 43
Hippisley-Coxe, A.D. 59
Hole, Christina 101
'Hooded Monk', the 74
Hunt, Robert 29

Ilfracombe 47

Johnson, Dr Samuel 15
Jolly Sailor inn 24
Judge Jeffreys 77, 78

Kentsford 94, 106
King Arthur 29, 96
Kirke, Colonel 80

Lady Jane Grey 47
Lanlavery Rock 42
Launceston 24, 25, 26
Leigh, William 86
Lew Trenchard 46, 52
Lewannick, 44
Lockley Manor, 81
Longleat 117, 119
Lower Penhale Farm 40, 44
Ludgershall 111
Lyme Regis 77, 79

Malmesbury, William 87
Maltravers, Sir John 90

Man in a Black Hat, The 15
Martyn's Ape 71
Martyn, Sir William 72
Miles, Ann 55
Mitchell, George 44
Mompesson, John 111
Monmouth Rebellion, the 80
Mortimer, Roger 89
Moyles Court, 82

Nash, Beau 2, 18
Neagle, Dame Anna 16
Newgate Prison 74

Oatway, Kate 49
'Old Doggett' 76
'Old Madam' 51

Padstow 30
Penfound Manor 20, 32, 33, 34
Penfounds, the 31
Perceval, Spencer 22
Peter, Philippa 40
Pigott, Thomas 102
Pinney, John 78
Popham, Sir John 116
Poundstock 30, 32, 34

Quarry Park 36
Queens Camel 98

Redruth 21
Rossiter, Philip 58
Roughtor 42
Ruddle, John 35

St Breock's Church 27
St Decuman's Church 106, 108
St Gennys, Simon de 31

St Margaret's Tower 60
Salisbury Cathedral 110
Sampford Peverell 54
Scorrier House 21
Scott, Sir Walter 115
Screaming Skull, the 77
Smith, John 89
Society for Psychical Research 102
Somerset 93
South Molton 64, 65
South Petherton 35
Stapleton Manor House 13
Stavordale Priory 98
Stoke Bishop 10
Sweet, Samuel 81

Tarrant Gunville 75
Taunton Castle 79
Tavistock 53
Theatre Royal 15, 17, 18
Thynne, Sir John 118
Tolland 98
Trebarfoot Manor 32

Trebarfoot, John 32
Trecarrel, Sir Henry 26
Tregeagle, Jan 27
Trematon Castle 21
Tucker, Kenneth and Doris 34
Turberville, 99
Turner, James 26

Vanbrugh, Sir John 75

Waylen, James 121
Wedgwood, Dr C.V. 7
Weeks, Matthew 40, 42, 44
Whitcombe Terrace 15
White Lady, the 14
Williams, John 21
Wiltshire 111
Woodberry, Martha 55
Woodchester Park Mansion 85
Wyndham, John 106

York Villa 16